SURE-HIRE
Cover Letters

SURE-HIRE Cover Letters

Robbie Miller Kaplan

Author of
101 Résumés for Sure-Hire Results and
The Whole Career Sourcebook

amacom
American Management Association
New York • Atlanta • Boston • Chicago • Kansas City • San Francisco • Washington, D.C.
Brussels • Tokyo • Toronto • Mexico City

This book is available at a special
discount when ordered in bulk quantities.
For information, contact Special Sales Department,
AMACOM, a division of American Management Association,
135 West 50th Street, New York, NY 10020.

This publication is designed to provide accurate and authoritative information in regard to the subject matter covered. It it sold with the
understanding that the publisher is not engaged in rendering legal,
accounting, or other professional service. If legal advice or other expert assistance is required, the services of a competent professional
person should be sought.

Library of Congress Cataloging-in-Publication Data

Kaplan, Robbie Miller.
    Sure-hire cover letters / Robbie Miller Kaplan.
        p.   cm.
      ISBN 0-8144-7854-9
        1. Cover letters.   2. Résumés (Employment)   I. Title.
    HF5383.K375   1994
    808'.06665—dc20   94-4274
                                                                  CIP

Printing number

10 9 8 7 6 5 4 3

Lovingly dedicated to
my mother and the memory of my father,
Jean and Sam Miller

Contents

Acknowledgments   ix

Introduction   xi

Part One   Basic Training   1

  1 Cover Letter Basics   3
    Why Write a Cover Letter?   3
    Letter Parts   6
    Cover Letter Ingredients   6
    Producing an Attractive Cover Letter   9
    Putting Your Cover Letter to Work   10
    Turning Possibilities Into Opportunities   12

  2 Types of Cover Letters   23
    Unsolicited Letters   23
    Advertisement Letters   24
    Referral Letters   25
    Résumé Letters   25

**Part Two   Before and After: Twenty-Five Cover Letter
              Makeovers   41**

Letters by Occupation Included in This Book

Accountant	66	Horticultural Assistant		86
Administrator, Assistant	142	Hotel Property Manager	30,	31
Administration, Director	82	Human Resources Manager		46
Administrative Assistant	50	Marketing Specialist		38
Association Executive	40	Mortgage Banking Settlement		
Auditor	37	Supervisor		32
Auditor, Chief	74	Nursing Director		102
Chief Financial Officer	98	Political Committee Member		62
College Dean	58	Project Manager, Real Estate		78
Computer Programmer	70	Public Relations Director		14
Computer Sales	134	Purchasing Agent		22
Contracts Administrator	110	Real Estate Developer		39
Controller, Assistant	138	Restaurant Manager		126
Credit and Collection Manager	94	Sales and Marketing, Vice President		33
Customer Service Supervisor	130	Store Manager, Retail		28
Data Processing Supervisor	90	Teacher, Elementary School		27
Development Director	118	Teacher, Secondary Math		36
Display Manager	20	Technical Trainer		54
Executive Assistant	122	Telecommunications Project		
Finance Assistant	29	Supervisor		26
Graphic Designer and Illustrator	106	Television Reporter		34
Health Services Coordinator	114	Travel Consultant		35
		Writer, Freelance		21

Letter Types Included in This Book

Unsolicited   20, 21, 22, 26, 27, 28, 29, 46, 54, 78, 86, 102, 106, 118, 122, 130, 142

Advertisement   30, 31

Referral   14, 35, 36, 37, 62

Résumé   38, 39, 40

Acknowledgments

Many thanks to my clients, friends, family, and colleagues, who graciously permitted me to use your cover letters.

A special thanks to Mary Fairchild, Betty McManus, and Judy Lynch for your input and manuscript review.

To my sister, Margie, for your ideas and suggestions.

And to Jim, Sam, and Julie, who never failed to support me, day or night. Thanks for all your help and for putting up with my writing schedule.

Introduction

Every day I work with clients who spend considerable time and money writing and producing their résumés. But when the time comes to write the accompanying cover letter, these same individuals exert little thought or effort and simply dash off a quick letter indicating an "enclosure." In fact, the importance of the cover letter to an effective job search campaign is often overlooked.

The job market is too competitive to ignore a proven strategy that provides a direct link to a potential employer. That's why I've written *Sure-Hire Cover Letters:* to show you how and why a cover letter can attract positive attention, make a vital connection, and provoke the recipient to learn more about you.

Like the flies you select to catch a fish, cover letters that get results should be appropriately alluring and provide the hook that makes the reader want to move on—to your résumé. If you make the catch, then the opportunity to sell yourself in person in a job interview is that much more likely to occur.

Let's work together. I'll show you how to make your cover letters sparkle and how to use them to expedite your job search. In Part One, I'll introduce you to all the basics: common letter formats, construction techniques, how to collect all the right materials, what each paragraph of the letter should include, and how to choose the right typeface and stationery.

I'll also give you many suggestions on how to use your cover letters effectively and efficiently, including tips on organizing the letter-mailing campaign.

A wise job seeker is one who creates a different letter for almost every job inquiry. Chapter 2 details the characteristics of the four basic cover letters: unsolicited, advertisement, referral, and résumé. You'll find examples of each type, with suggestions about their use.

Finally, Part Two presents twenty-five before-and-after cover letters, examples that demonstrate what makes one cover letter a success and another a failure. For each letter, I have highlighted problems and suggested improvements. I invite you to read and consider each one. You are certain to find any number of ideas that you can take and use right away.

Part One
Basic Training

1
Cover Letter Basics

Jeff W., a participant in one of my job search workshops, had been out of work for a year and was supporting himself with temporary assignments. He'd sent out over 100 résumés and cover letters, yet hadn't received a single nibble. He'd practiced his interview techniques, but was never given an opportunity to use them.

Jeff knew he had the qualifications and tenacity to make a contribution, but his résumé and cover letter failed to deliver that message. I helped Jeff rewrite his résumé, and together we developed several cover letters that he could tailor for specific opportunities. Two weeks later, Jeff happily reported that ten letters and résumés had netted two job interviews. After selling himself on paper, he finally had a chance to sell himself in person.

Like many people I've worked with, Jeff had been spinning his wheels trying to meet prospective employers. He learned the hard way that although there are many facets of the job search, success hinges on making initial contact with employers.

Why Write a Cover Letter?

A cover letter is a business letter directed to a prospective employer that indicates your interest in employment with an organization. Usually it accompanies your résumé, serving to introduce it. Since résumés that arrive without a cover letter are rarely read, think of the résumé and cover letter as a team.

A cover letter tells a prospective employer a lot about you, both by what you choose to include and exclude and by whether you pay attention to detail. It shows how professional you are and how well you communicate.

Hiring managers use cover letters to screen likely candidates from the unlikely. An enticing letter encourages them to review your résumé. Your résumé should be very striking, but if your cover letter doesn't tempt the reader, your résumé may not get a glance.

You can often use the same résumé for all jobs, but your cover letter must be tailored and directed for each specific position so that the reader thinks it was written solely for him or her. Each letter must highlight the qualifications related to the specific job opportunity you pursue. Optimally, each letter should reflect how your qualifications fit and mesh with the requirements for each job you seek. Make the recruiter's job easy and get results by addressing all the job requirements.

While the objective of your résumé is to make the employer want to meet you in person, the objective of your cover letter is to get your résumé read. Here are twelve basics to keep in mind:

1. Type all letters; handwritten letters are unacceptable. A personnel specialist once showed me a letter and résumé she had received—written in calligraphy. Commenting on the letter's beauty, she said she wished she had a need for a calligrapher. However, neither of us bothered to review the text to see what kind of job the applicant was seeking.

2. Use single spacing for the text and double spacing between paragraphs.

3. To achieve a professional and neat appearance, use full justification; this produces even margins by aligning the text at the right as well as at the left. Many word processing programs let you hyphenate words that don't fit. Hyphenation can be turned on or off. Consult your reference manual and choose your preference.

4. Allow one-inch margins at top, bottom, and sides of the letter. For a balanced, sleek look, use your software's "center page" feature to center the text vertically between the top and bottom margins.

5. Address each letter to a specific individual, and include his or her name and job title in the inside address. If you are sending an unsolicited letter, research at the library or call the company to find out whom to send it to. If you are responding to a classified advertisement that does not include the name of the person to send it to, call the organization and identify the recipient. Above all else, make sure to spell the person's name correctly and use his or her correct title.

6. If you don't know what courtesy title a woman prefers, use *Ms.* If you are unable to determine the individual's gender, omit the courtesy title and begin the letter like this:

Kelley Smith:
or
Dear Kelley Smith:

7. Date and sign the letter.

8. Include your telephone number (don't forget the area code), either in the return address or in your closing paragraph.

9. Abbreviate the state name on both the inside and outside address, using acceptable post office abbreviations. If you include your address, abbreviate the state name as well. But it is permissible either to spell out or to abbreviate the state name on your letterhead. And remember, state names are always spelled out in the text of your letter. Consult the following table for the abbreviations recommended by the U.S. Postal Service.

AL	Alabama		**MT**	Montana
AK	Alaska		**NE**	Nebraska
AR	Arkansas		**NH**	New Hampshire
AZ	Arizona		**NV**	Nevada
CA	California		**NJ**	New Jersey
CZ	Canal Zone		**NM**	New Mexico
CO	Colorado		**NY**	New York
CT	Connecticut		**NC**	North Carolina
DE	Delaware		**ND**	North Dakota
DC	District of Columbia		**OH**	Ohio
FL	Florida		**OK**	Oklahoma
GA	Georgia		**OR**	Oregon
GU	Guam		**PA**	Pennsylvania
HI	Hawaii		**PR**	Puerto Rico
ID	Idaho		**RI**	Rhode Island
IL	Illinois		**SC**	South Carolina
IN	Indiana		**SD**	South Dakota
IA	Iowa		**TN**	Tennessee
KS	Kansas		**TX**	Texas
KY	Kentucky		**UT**	Utah
LA	Louisiana		**VT**	Vermont
ME	Maine		**VA**	Virginia
MD	Maryland		**VI**	Virgin Islands
MA	Massachusetts		**WA**	Washington
MI	Michigan		**WV**	West Virginia
MN	Minnesota		**WI**	Wisconsin
MS	Mississippi		**WY**	Wyoming
MO	Missouri			

10. Include the following notation when enclosing items:

Enclosure
Encl.
or
Enc.

If more than one enclosure is included, specify the number:

Enclosures (2)

11. Follow basic rules for numbers. It is usual to spell out numbers from 1 through 10, using figures for 11 and over. Always spell out a number that begins a sentence. Be consistent and follow the same style—for related numbers—in a paragraph. Check for special rules in a business-writing reference book.

12. Consult reference book, dictionaries, and thesauruses for rules on grammar, usage, business-writing principles, word choice, and spelling.

Letter Parts

Your letters must follow accepted business-letter principles and formats. Your letter set-up—space between elements, paragraph indents, placement of addresses, salutations, and closes—must be consistent and clear because you don't want to give a recruiter any reason to discard your letter, and your résumé. Exhibit 1 shows all the basic elements. The most appropriate business-letter formats are the block, semiblock, semiblock indented, and block indented. All four are acceptable, and the choice is yours. Examples of these are shown in Exhibit 2.

Cover Letter Ingredients

Hiring managers want to hire you—if you meet the job requirements and can convey the fact that you do. I recently asked recruiters and hiring managers what they looked for in a cover letter and they all agreed that they wanted you to tell them how you fit the bill. Many people do meet job requirements, but their letters are bland, lacking the essential ingredients and seasonings that make appetizing letters.

Have you ever experimented with a new recipe, only to find when you started cooking that you were missing an ingredient? Maybe you didn't have the time to run to the store, so you made a substitution or continued on without the ingredient. Chances are the meal didn't turn out as well as it would have if you assembled all your ingredients and then began cooking.

Writing a cover letter is a lot like cooking. You need the ingredients (the text of your letter) and a recipe, or plan, for putting them all together.

The following questions will help you collect the ingredients for your letter. Exhibit 3 shows how job-seeker Shelley Charles used the worksheet to collect information for her cover letter.

(text continues on page 12)

Exhibit 1. Basic business-letter set-up.

Writer's address   28 Liberty Street
Pontiac, MI 48341
(313) 444-XXXX

[Spacing varies,
usually 2-4 spaces]

Date   November 14, 1993

[4 spaces]
Mr. John Jones
Personnel Director   Inside address
ABC Company
85 Main Street
Pontiac, MI 48341
[2 spaces]
Dear Mr. Jones: Salutation
[2 spaces]

    Peter Smith suggested I contact you concerning your search for a Director of Public Relations. My six years of progressive public relations experience qualifies me for this position.
[2 spaces]   Body of letter
I have worked with both non-profit and corporate organizations, developing an expertise in cultivating local and national media contacts.
[2 spaces]

    New projects and ideas are particularly exciting to me, and I enjoy transforming concepts into reality. Additionally, I have excellent interpersonal and management skills, and I interface effectively at all organizational levels.
[2 spaces]

    I am interested in the challenge your position presents and would like to meet with you to discuss my credentials and your requirements. I look forward to speaking with you.
[2 spaces]

Complimentary close   Sincerely yours,

[4 spaces]

Close   Dillon Thompson

[2 spaces]
Encl.

Exhibit 2. The four business-letter formats.

Full Block
All text is set flush against the left-hand margin.

_____
_____
_____

_____

_____
_____
_____

_____ :

_____
_____

_____
_____

_____ ,

_____

Encl.

Semiblock

The date and writer's address usually align at the center of the page. The complimentary close and the writer's name align under the address.

_____
_____
_____

_____

_____
_____
_____

_____ :

_____
_____

_____
_____

_____ ,

_____

Encl.

(continues)

Exhibit 2 *(continued)***.**

Semiblock Indented
The date, complimentary close, and the writer's name are set on a tab and align with each other. The first line of each paragraph is also indented.

_____
_____
_____

_____

_____
_____
_____

_____ :

_____
_____
_____
_____

_____ ,

_____

Encl.

Block Indented

The date, complimentary close, and the writer's name are set flush left. The first line of each paragraph is indented.

_____

_____

_____

_____

_____

_____

_____

_____ :

    _____
_____ .

    _____
_____
_____ .

_____ ,

_____

Encl.

1. *What's your message? or What's the purpose of your letter?*

_____

_____

_____

Possible Answers:

"I'm interested in pursuing an engineering career with ABC Electronics."

"Jan Dime suggested I contact you concerning teaching opportunities."

"I've heard about an opening in the accounting department through the National Capital Area Accounting Forum."

"I'd like to apply for the editorial position advertised in the June 13, 1993, *New York Times.*"

2. *What can you offer an employer that's special?*

_____

_____

_____

Possible Answers:

"Seven years' experience writing provocative articles on women's health issues."

"Track record in retaining and building a strong client base."

"Technical expertise and the ability to fix anything mechanical."

"Commitment and loyalty to cleaning up the environment."

3. *What are your qualifications and accomplishments? (Address all job requirements.)*

_____

_____

_____

_____

_____

Possible Answers:

"Twenty years' experience in secondary and college-level education as an administrator and professor. Youngest faculty member to ever receive tenure."

"Excellent office support skills resulting in progressive promotions to Executive Assistant."

"Expertise in desktop publishing. Three years of experience creating and producing newsletters for four nonprofit organizations."

4. *How can you demonstrate your achievements and results?*

_____

_____

_____

Possible Answers:

"I can contribute to your programming efforts by creating test data, performing user acceptance testing and documentation, and supporting production systems."

"My experience in acute settings and expertise in effectively managing emergency situations will make me a valuable addition to your health care team."

"Consistently exceed sales performance goals. Awarded Sales Representative of the Month for six consecutive months, 1993."

5. *What outcome do you want from the letter?*

_____

_____

_____

Possible Answers:

"I'd like to demonstrate in person my enthusiasm and interest in the teaching position."

"I would like to meet with Mr. Smith to discuss how I can make a contribution at XYZ Corporation."

"A personal meeting to discuss how my qualifications meet your requirements."

"An opportunity to discuss how I can help your department reach its goal."

Helpful Starters

Shelley Charles and other job seekers have found the following resources useful in identifying and expressing their qualifications, strengths, and contributions.

- Phrases from prior performance appraisals, letters of commendation, and letters of recommendation
- Current and past job descriptions and standards of performance that clearly express job expectations and responsibilities
- Desirable characteristics and requested skills for similar jobs advertised in the employment classified section of the newspaper
- Newspaper editorials and business sections to help craft paragraphs about your industry, occupation, or the economy

Exhibit 3. Shelley Charles' cover-letter ingredients for a Display Manager position.

1. *What's your message? or What's the purpose of your letter?*

   "I am interested in a Display Manager position with Hall & Young."

2. *What can you offer an employer that's special?*

   "I transform merchandise into fashion excitement."

3. *What are your qualifications and accomplishments? (Address all job requirements.)*

   "Six years' experience stimulating and increasing sales by creating captivating window and department displays.

   "A talent for coordinating individual pieces into unique combinations and ensembles.

   "Bachelor of Arts degree in Fashion Merchandising from Fashion Institute of Technology."

4. *How can you demonstrate your achievements and results?*

   "A proven record promoting merchandise and products through innovative themes and staging."

5. *What outcome do you want from the letter?*

   "I'd like a personal interview where I can demonstrate my commitment and desire to contribute to the organization."

Here is a standard cover letter recipe that you can adjust to your taste by modifying the format, organization, or special effects. You can begin working on your cover letter by taking the ingredients (the answers to the questions) and organizing them into appropriate paragraphs.

1st Paragraph:	The introductory or opening paragraph states the purpose of your letter. Are you responding to an employment advertisement? Did someone refer you to the organization? Are you intrigued by its products or services? Arouse the reader's interest now, and he or she will want to read further.
2nd Paragraph:	This transitional paragraph expands on your opening by including your experience, education/training, and other credentials that meet the job requirements.
3rd Paragraph:	Here you can familiarize the reader with your accomplishments, e.g., increased membership, decreased expenditures. Use a sentence or two to explain how you fit the position and what you'll bring to it, e.g., enthusiasm, dedication, commitment.
4th Paragraph:	This paragraph ties into the first by restating your interest in the organization and/or position, stating your availability, and making a request to meet or speak about the job or opportunities.

Once your letter is roughed out, edit, rewrite, and reorganize your sentences until you're satisfied with their clarity and construction. Check for grammatical errors, redundancies, misspelled words, and overall accuracy. See Exhibit 4 for how Shelley Charles put her letter together.

Producing an Attractive Cover Letter

Presentation is as important as content. Let's consider a number of factors. First, your letter must be produced on a typewriter, word processor, or word processing software. A word processor or software is preferable, since you can make changes easily, make the letter graphically interesting, and store the information for future use.

Select a print style (font) that is easy to read and professional in appearance. Avoid script, italics, Old English, calligraphy, or any print type that is unprofessional or detracts from your content. Make sure the type size is readable. While it is common to use 10- , 12- , and even 14-point type for a résumé, a cover letter is a business letter, so use the standard 12-point type.

Exhibit 4. Shelley Charles' cover letter.

Shelley Charles
11 Elm Avenue
Buffalo, New York 14222
(716) 433-XXXX

September 18, 1993

Hall & Young
Mr. Horace Timmons
Personnel Manager
4778 Second Street
Buffalo, NY 14220

Dear Mr. Timmons:

Could your organization use a skilled fashion professional with a flair for transforming merchandise into fashion excitement? If so, consider me for a Display Manager position with Hall & Young.

My qualifications, as outlined in the enclosed résumé, include:

- Six years' experience stimulating and increasing sales by creating captivating window and department displays.
- Proven record promoting merchandise and products through innovative themes and staging.
- Talent for coordinating individual pieces into unique combinations and ensembles.
- Bachelor of Arts in Fashion Merchandising from Fashion Institute of Technology.

I am ready for a new challenge and would like to meet with you to demonstrate my commitment and desire to make a contribution to Hall & Young. I will call you to set up an appointment.

Thank you for your consideration.

Sincerely,

Shelley Charles

Encl.

You Must Proofread!

Any mistake, whether it concerns spelling, grammar, punctuation, or poor word choice, can knock you out of the running. You've spent too much time and effort writing your letter to lose out because of errors. If your typewriter, word processor, or computer software has a spelling checker, use it. But don't rely on it; it will bypass words that are spelled correctly but are not the correct word. For example, if you mistakenly type *manger* instead of *manager*, the spelling checker will accept *manger*.

Choosing Stationery

You'll achieve a very professional appearance by producing your cover letters and résumés on the same paper. Choose 8 ½- by 11-inch twenty-four-pound stationery, 100 percent rag (best quality) to 25 percent rag (good quality). Stationery supply stores and copy/print shops carry a wide range of paper and envelopes. I tend to be conservative when it comes to color and recommend white, off-white, buff, ivory, or beige; the most risqué I get is pale grey. Avoid marbled, mottled paper, regardless of color; it's hard to read and photocopies poorly (employers often make photocopies of cover letters to distribute to other hiring managers).

Personalized stationery gives your cover letters a very polished, professional look. You can create your own business letterhead if you have access to desktop publishing or word processing software with desktop publishing capabilities. Another option is to center your address and phone number at the top of the page. See examples on pages 46 and 58.

I recommend that you purchase envelopes to match your paper, but use them only for sending follow-up letters and thank you notes. To ensure that your cover letter and résumé arrive unfolded and unwrinkled, send them in a 9- by 12-inch envelope.

Putting Your Cover Letter to Work

With your appealing and alluring letters in hand, ensure the best results by developing a strategy for using them. Decide how much, or what percentage, of your time you'll direct to finding job opportunities. For example: 40 percent for networking, 25 percent for referrals, 10 percent for employment classified advertisements, and 25 percent for direct applications.

Sally H., a recent successful job seeker, took that approach to great effect. "I used unsolicited, referral, and advertisement letters in my recent job search. It was hard for me to see any progress or maintain any sense of control when I randomly sent out a letter." Sally found she got the best results when she was organized and set goals for her search. "I developed a schedule and allotted times for different types of letters, calls, meetings and interviews. It was a lot easier motivating myself to achieve my goals and assessing my progress when I had something concrete to measure myself by."

Getting Organized

What worked for Sally will work for you too. Design a strategy that suits your needs and job search goals. Each of us functions best in our own orderly—or not so orderly—environment. The following tips will help you organize your job search:

1. Keep a record of every letter you mail, including such information as date mailed, company or box number, contact name, phone number, follow-up dates (several columns), and results. Log in every letter sent, whether it's a response to an advertisement, referral, or unsolicited letter.
2. Print extra copies or make photocopies of every letter you send and store them in file folders (labeled for each type of letter) or a three-ring binder. When you respond to an advertisement from a newspaper or professional journal, attach it to your photocopy.
3. Schedule mailings to fit your daily routine. Try mailing responses to the Sunday employment classified advertisements on one particular day and unsolicited and referral letters on another.
4. If you're doing a bulk mailing and you think it will take you two weeks to complete it, date all the letters with the future completion date. Mail all letters together when completed. If you mail a letter to yourself you'll have an idea of when your letters reached their destination.
5. Always follow up a letter with a phone call after you allow the letter a day or two to travel through the office mail system.

The Follow-Up Call

I have seen so many job seekers exert great effort seeking out job leads, researching potential employers, writing and mailing dozens of letters only to stagnate in the job search because they failed to follow up their letters with a phone call. Don't make the same mistake.

The success of your job search is directly correlated to how well you follow up your letters. Employers do not have the time or the interest to respond to every letter they receive. And so, it is in your best interest to follow up every letter you send with a phone call requesting a personal meeting or interview.

Since these phone calls aren't easy to make, consider preparing a script. You will be more relaxed if you know in advance what you want to say. Here's an example you can modify to meet your needs.

"Hello Mr. Smith. This is Robbie Kaplan. I'm following up on a letter I sent you last week concerning job opportunities within your organization [*pause; give him a chance to respond*].

"I'd like to set up an appointment with you to discuss my qualifications and your needs [*pause*]."

If Mr. Smith says no thanks, try to get something positive out of the exchange. For instance, you could ask if he knows of any job opportunities inside or outside his organization or if he could recommend someone with knowledge about job openings. Remember, nothing ventured, nothing gained. Follow-up phone calls are a great way to get referrals, and it's a lot easier contacting someone when you can say, "Mr. Smith suggested I give you a call concerning accounting opportunities."

You'll find it most effective to make at least ten calls at a time. You develop a rhythm when making a number of calls and become more confident and at ease the more calls you make. Begin with the least risky/least wanted and save jobs or contacts of greatest interest for last. Each individual you reach and each successful encounter will buoy your spirits.

If you make your calls either between 8:30 A.M. and 9:00 A.M. or between 4:30 P.M. and 5:00 P.M., you'll catch more people at their desks. If you reach a secretary and find the contact is not available, advise him or her that you'll call back. Or leave your name and number and say explicitly that you're following up on correspondence with Mr. Smith. If you reach PhoneMail® or an answering machine, leave a message detailing your name, that you're following up on correspondence, that you'd like a return call, and where you can be reached.

If within one week you don't receive a return call, place another phone call. People are busy and don't always give these types of calls priority.

Turning Possibilities Into Opportunities

The most successful job searches are directed by positive thinking. You can turn negatives into positives by being as proactive and persistent as possible. For example, if an organization turns you down and you're still interested, locate a hiring manager or individual in another division.

Melanie K. responded to a newspaper advertisement for a Special Education Teacher and received a form-letter reply that the position had been filled by a more qualified candidate. Six months later, the organization readvertised the position. Melanie, refusing to be discouraged, wrote a different cover letter but used the same résumé, and this time she received a call for a job interview.

If you've heard of an appealing job or seen one advertised, and, for whatever reason, the fit is not quite right, contact the organization anyway and offer your services in another capacity (see Exhibit 5).

Exhibit 5. Response offering services in a different capacity from what was suggested in the ad.

---

2 Rose Lane
Harrison, New York 10528
(914) 222-XXXX

January 2, 1994

College Books, Inc.
10 Broadway
12th Floor
New York, NY 10038

Dear Ms. Williams:

Although I do not have experience for the Managing Editor position you advertised in The New York Times, I am interested in becoming a free-lance writer for your company.

As an educator and writer, I developed a wide variety of training programs and workshops for diverse audiences. I also wrote successful grant proposals, researched and created innovative curriculum projects, and generated and gathered pertinent information for annual program evaluation reports.

Most recently, I wrote a health textbook for second grade students. The enclosed resumé highlights my accomplishments.

I would like the opportunity to meet with you to discuss my credentials and your requirements.

Sincerely,

Joanna Joseph

Encl.

Being proactive also means dealing with a pending layoff. If your organization is downsizing and you're facing a layoff, ask your immediate supervisor to write you a letter of introduction. Many organizations, faced with terminating qualified individuals, are willing not only to write letters but direct and address them to appropriate organizations.

These letters (see Exhibit 6) are written on your employer's stationery, and either you or your employer supplies the organizations and contact names. If your employer plans to address them "To Whom It May Concern," ask if they can be personalized if you supply names and addresses.

Exhibit 6. Example of a letter of introduction from an organization experiencing an overall staff cutback.

ABC Company
67th Highway
Ft. Lauderdale, FL 33395

January 2, 1994

Ms. Rosalind Thompson
Health Care U.S.A.
7880 Sunny Boulevard
Ft. Lauderdale, FL 33394

Dear Ms. Thompson:

I want to give you my recommendation for Larry Long, who is an employee with ABC Company. Mr. Long is a Purchasing Agent at Headquarters in Ft. Lauderdale, Florida.

Mr. Long has been a member of ABC's purchasing staff since January 1990. I have found him to be an extremely competent and conscientious employee and feel he would be an asset to any organization.

Our purchasing program entails working with several hospitals to establish common purchasing programs in medical supplies through national contracts and dealing with miscellaneous bulk purchases outside of the medical supplies area. Mr. Long's interpersonal skills and knowledge of purchasing and negotiation has been valuable in performing these tasks.

I regret that due to ABC Company's effort to reduce a large budget deficit, I have been forced to terminate Mr. Long's employment as part of an overall staff cutback.

If you have any questions about Mr. Long's abilities to assist your organization, please contact me at (407) 777-XXXX.

Sincerely,

Marsha Mitt
General Manager

MM/jk

2
Types of Cover Letters

You may be able to get away with one good blue suit, but you're going to need a wardrobe of letters to run a successful job search. What follows is an introduction to four types of cover letters: unsolicited, advertisement, referral, and résumé. A wide range of examples follow the descriptions, each from different occupations and experience levels. There are sure to be examples here that relate to you.

Unsolicited Letters

The happiest employees are those who find organizations that are in sync with their personalities and values. Why not do some research to identify organizations you'd like to work for and send an unsolicited letter, presenting yourself as a potential employee? The unsolicited letter has an added benefit: There's less competition when you're not applying with the pack!

Put your investigative skills to use in tracking down likely candidates. Read the business sections of local and national newspapers, keeping an eye open for news of contract awards, recent moves, acquisitions, and who's moving where. Local business calendars, the Yellow Pages of the phone directory, business and professional magazines and journals, and local directories of business and industry all provide information. Consider organizations that produce products or services that you find handy or useful. Ask friends and contacts about likely prospects.

Once you find an organization that interests you, do additional research to identify the appropriate hiring manager, either through directories, networking, or calling the organization directly. Confirm the correct spelling of the individual's name and his or her exact job title.

Employers get a lot of unsolicited mail, most of which ends up in the wastepaper basket. To make sure your letter is read, write a catchy opening and create an appealing format.

23

Exhibits 7, 8, 9, and 10 on pages 26–29 present interesting examples of unsolicited letters.

Advertisement Letters

While advertisements in the newspaper employment classified section are the most common form of job listings, you'll also find them in professional journals, professional magazines, association newsletters, organization newsletters, job banks, job phone lines (hotlines), online information services, and computer bulletin boards.

Approximately 10 percent of all jobs are found through the classifieds. Despite this low number, this is the most frequently used job-lead source. As a result, classified advertisements generate thousands of responses. In other words, your letter will have lots of competition, so your response must be written and formatted to catch attention.

Many job seekers waste too much time using this method in their job search. If you do choose to use the newspaper ads, invest no more than 10 percent of your job search time.

The Sunday employment classified section of a local or national paper is the most complete source of advertised job openings. Read through it in its entirety; similar jobs can be listed under different headings and are not always cross-referenced. For example, personnel jobs are listed under "human resources," "personnel," "training," and "municipal" (if for local government). Also look under industry headings like "health care," where functional jobs will be listed as well.

As you work your way through the listings, circle interesting jobs with a highlighting marker. When you've identified the ads you want to respond to, cut them out and highlight the job requirements, both required and desired.

If the advertisement names the organization but doesn't provide an individual name or requests that inquiries be sent to *Personnel Director,* call and ask for a name (and spelling) so you can direct your letter more personally. If you can't tell if the individual is a man or a woman, use the full name: *Dear Robbie Kaplan.* If no organization or name is listed, address the letter to *Dear Employer.* This is more contemporary than *Sir, Madam,* or *Gentlemen.*

Underscore the titles of publications. This type of letter is not followed up with a phone call. Your fourth paragraph should only state your availability and interest.

Some ads request a salary history or salary requirements. Recruiters I've discussed this with say that they need this information in order to determine whether you fit into the job's salary range. However, I believe you put yourself at a disadvantage in revealing what your requirements are without knowing the salary range. You must be aware, though, that if you don't include salary history or requirements when responding to an ad, you could exclude yourself from consideration. It's your decision.

Get an edge on the competition by mailing your letters Sunday or Monday. If that doesn't give you enough time to craft well-written letters, don't rush the process; mail the letters later in the week. Hiring managers differ on letter timing. When they're under pressure to fill jobs, they like them in by Tuesday to make the first interview cut. If a closing date is listed, most wait until that date to review all letters and resumés. One manager believes he gets better letters later in the week; possibly the letters reflect the time taken to research and prepare.

On pages 30–34 you'll find five examples of letters responding to newspaper advertisements (Exhibits 11, 12, 13, 14, and 15). The first two letters are written in response to the same ad for a Property Manager but show different levels of experience. Note the differences and similarities (one sentence is identical).

Referral Letters

You're probably familiar with the expression, "It's not what you know, but whom you know." The hiring process is time-consuming and risky. Referrals minimize the risk for recruiters. If a recruiter knows and is comfortable with the work and values of the person referring you, chances are he or she will assume you have similar work ethics and values.

Begin your referral letter by identifying the individual who recommended that you write. The recipient should personally know this individual and so be able to quickly make a connection. Follow this opening statement with the ingredients listed in Chapter 1. Three examples of referral letters follow (see Exhibits 16, 17, and 18 on pages 35–37).

Résumé Letters

There may be times when sending a résumé with your cover letter just won't do. For instance, if you are applying to a competitor of your current employer, you may have to keep some information confidential. In this and other cases, a résumé letter may best fit your needs.

A résumé letter is a one-page summary that outlines your accomplishments and training/education. Since it's a combination résumé and cover letter, it is longer than the usual cover letter. Still, it follows all the basic principles. Three résumé-letter examples follow on pages 38–40 (Exhibits 19, 20, and 21).

Exhibit 7.

39 Kennedy Lane
New Orleans, Louisiana 70110
(504) 721-XXXX

January 2, 1994

Communication Systems, Inc.
One Glade Way
New Orleans, LA 70115

Dear Mr. Beam:

It is increasingly difficult to find qualified individuals to install and maintain cable systems.

During my ten years in the telecommunications field, I have developed a specialty in large cable designs. My qualifications include:

• Technical expertise and the unique ability to find innovative solutions
• Quick and accurate engineering and cost estimates at less than 1% installed cost variance
• Ability to identify and meet customer requirements resulting in satisfied customers and a quality reputation

In my present position, I supervise subcontractor cable projects from 100 to 3,000 lines, estimating material costs and providing building, plant, and campus cable engineering and layout. Additional qualifications are highlighted in the enclosed résumé.

Mr. Beam, I'm interested in meeting with you and discussing opportunities at Communication Systems, Inc. I'll give you a call next week to schedule an appointment.

Thank you for your time.

Sincerely yours,

Nancy Porter

Encl.

Exhibit 8.

---

98 Vista Boulevard
Armonk, NY 10504
(914) 744-XXXX

February 4, 1994

Bergen County Public Schools
Dr. Caswell, Director of Personnel
Wishfull Lane
Paramus, NJ 01652

Dear Dr. Caswell:

Could your organization benefit from the services of a hardworking, organized elementary school teacher, dedicated to innovative teaching?

I would like to put my skills to use in a teaching position in Bergen
County, and I'm willing to invest the time and effort to motivate your
pupils to reach their potential.

My qualifications, as detailed in the enclosed résumé, include:

- Five years of teaching experience in the Westchester County
  Schools, third and fourth grades.
- Master of Arts degree in Elementary Education.
- Permanent Certification, New York State, Elementary Grades N-6.
- Excellent communication skills and ability to establish rapport
  with administrators, teachers, and students.

I plan to relocate to Bergen County in March. I will be in the area the
week of February 20-27 and will call you to schedule an appointment.

I look forward to speaking with you soon.

                              Sincerely,

                              Paula Black

Enclosure

Exhibit 9.

---

932 Stone Ridge Lane
Boston, Massachusetts 02110
(617) 522-XXXX

December 15, 1993

ABC Retailers
Ms. Holloway
Vice President, Human Resources
76 High Street
Hingham, MA 02043

Dear Ms. Holloway:

Your organization impresses me both by the quality of your merchandise and the high level of customer service. I'm interested in joining the team at ABC Retailers as a Store Manager.

For the past five years, I have held progressively more senior management positions at a chain of national clothing stores. I have a flair for selecting merchandise and motivating staff members to meet customer needs.

Most recently, my store has achieved regional recognition as #1 in increased profits. I have diligently trained my staff and am proud of our high degree of customer satisfaction.

I would like the opportunity to meet with you in person to convey my enthusiasm and interest in joining your organization. I will call you next week to schedule a meeting.

Sincerely,

Bill Bones

Encl.

Exhibit 10.

1200 Lilac Lane
Chicago, IL 60606
(312) 844-XXXX

January 2, 1994

Mr. Henry Hudson
Controller
Better Books
45 Crystal Court
Riverside, CA 92501

Dear Mr. Hudson:

Recent articles in <u>Inc.</u> magazine highlight your organization as one of the fastest growing book chains in the West. A position in your Financial Operations department would enable me to combine my passion for reading with my degree in finance.

I will graduate from the University of Chicago in June and plan on relocating to the Riverside area.

During the week of January 29, I will be visiting Riverside and would like to speak with you concerning opportunities in your organization.

I will call to arrange a meeting and look forward to speaking with you.

Yours truly,

Michael Krum

Encl.

Exhibit 11.

---

41 Fifteenth Street
Longwood, Florida 32750
(305) 367-XXXX

December 27, 1993

Tampa Management Corp.
15 Beach Way
Tampa, FL 33688

Dear Director of Human Resources:

Your advertisement for a Property Manager in Sunday's <u>Tampa Tribune</u> challenged and excited me. I'd love to work with your management team in making this newly renovated property a success!

My qualifications and diversified background include both hands-on and management experience with front office and housekeeping operations. The following accomplishments highlight some of my strengths and abilities:

- Consistently meet/exceed the needs and requirements of guests. Perform beyond job expectations to satisfy guest needs.
- Adeptly utilize computer registration system; train new employees on computerized system and customer relations.
- Effectively and efficiently resolve guest problems and complaints.
- Skillfully initiated and conducted an employment satisfaction survey. Reduced employee turnover and increased satisfaction by implementing employment procedures.

I'd like to meet with you in person to further discuss my qualifications and your needs.

Sincerely yours,

Harriet Hayes

Encl.

> **Hotel**
> **PROPERTY MANAGER**
> **Sheraton Inn**
> Excellent opportunity for dynamic hotel professional to join the management team of this newly renovated 125-room property in Tampa, FL. This position requires a combination of hands-on skills in the areas of front office management and housekeeping operations. The successful candidate will possess computerized front desk skills and a proven record in the areas of guest satisfaction, employee relations and leadership abilities. Submit resume to:
> Tampa Management Corp.
> Director of H.R.
> 15 Beach Way
> Tampa, FL 33688

Exhibit 12.

9007 Church Street
Jacksonville, Florida 32240
(904) 278-XXXX

December 27, 1993

Tampa Management Corp.
15 Beach Way
Tampa, FL 33688

Dear Director of Human Resources:

Your company has always impressed me, and I was excited to see your advertisement for a Property Manager in Sunday's Tampa Tribune. I'd love to work with your management team in making this newly renovated property a success!

I will graduate from the University of Miami in January with a degree in Hotel Management. I'm highly motivated and have a strong interest in building a career in the hotel industry.

My excellent interpersonal skills and a proven record of effectively resolving problems and exceeding job expectations make me a viable job candidate. My experience is more intensive than extensive. I have worked as a Guest Services Representative for Holiday Inn, where I adeptly used a computer system to register guests and reserve rooms and continually satisfied guest requirements. For my performance, I was recognized as "Employee of the Month" in October, which led to an opportunity to act as Assistant Manager in November.

If you're looking for a diligent and hard worker, look no further. I'm available to meet with you in person to discuss my qualifications and your needs.

Sincerely,

Gregory Young

Encl.

Exhibit 13.

---

734 Laurel Ridge Road
Omaha, Nebraska 68140
(402) 622-XXXX

September 1, 1993

Acme Mortgage Company
89 Plains Place
Omaha, NE 68144

Dear Employer:

I would like to put my experience and skills to use as the Settlement Supervisor you advertised for in the August 30 World-Herald.

My background, as outlined in the enclosed résumé, includes extensive experience preparing legal documents for settlement and performing closing reviews of Conventional, FHA, and VA loans.

In my current position as Settlement Supervisor, I manage a settlement department for a mortgage office with annual proceeds of $225 million, handling all aspects of residential loan settlements and working effectively with attorneys, appraisers, and realtors.

Excellent communication skills coupled with the ability to perform effectively under pressure while meeting deadlines have contributed to my progress and success.

Thank you for taking the time to review my credentials. I look forward to meeting you to further discuss my qualifications.

Sincerely yours,

Bruce Reed

Enclosure

Mortgage Banking
SETTLEMENT SUPERVISOR
The successful candidate will perform closing reviews of mortgage loans and prepare legal documents for settlement. Candidates must have 2–3 years' closing experience and a knowledge of Conventional, FHA and VA loans. Strong communication skills, the ability to meet deadlines and work under pressure also required.

Interested and qualified individuals please send resumes to:
   Acme Mortgage Company
   89 Plains Place
   Omaha, NE 68144

Exhibit 14.

75 Ortega Court
San Diego, California 92110
(714) 487-XXXX

October 5, 1993

United Plastics
San Buenavista Boulevard
Culver City, CA 90230

Dear Employer:

I was delighted to see your advertisement for a V. P. Sales & Marketing in the Los Angeles *Times* on October 3rd. I was struck by the similarity between your requirements and my background.

My extensive experience in sales and marketing management has resulted in expanded markets and increased corporate profits. What I've done for my previous employers, I can do for you.

Sales and Profits

Assumed responsibility for Southwest U.S. region of office equipment business. Increased sales from an initial flat $10 million level to $21 million level.
Generated 25% return on revenue, the highest in the company, contributing an estimated 22% of total company profits.

Staff Development

Reorganized sales operation; expanded staff from 25 to 53. Developed and conducted effective training programs; reduced staff turnover to minimum. Was recognized for "superior leadership skills."

Business Development

Highly successful in developing new business opportunities. Created effective marketing and advertising programs specifically designed to increase sales in commercial and international markets.

I am interested in taking on a new challenge and excited about the possibility of joining the United Plastics team. I would like to meet with you and discuss how I can help your organization reach its sales and marketing goals.

Sincerely,

Betty Blake

Encl.

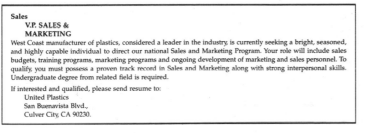

Sales
V.P. SALES &
MARKETING
West Coast manufacturer of plastics, considered a leader in the industry, is currently seeking a bright, seasoned, and highly capable individual to direct our national Sales and Marketing Program. Your role will include sales budgets, training programs, marketing programs and ongoing development of marketing and sales personnel. To qualify, you must possess a proven track record in Sales and Marketing along with strong interpersonal skills. Undergraduate degree from related field is required.

If interested and qualified, please send resume to:
    United Plastics
    San Buenavista Blvd.,
    Culver City, CA 90230.

Exhibit 15.

---

65 Greyhound Street
Coral Gables, Florida 33134
(305) 884-XXXX

July 5, 1993

CABLE USA
Ms. Harriet Wilson
45 Fourth Avenue
New York, NY 10021

Dear Ms. Wilson:

Your advertisement for a Television Reporter-Spanish Language is an exact match for my quali-fications. My five years of experience as a television reporter for WXKZ Miami, a Spanish-language station, parallels your advertised requirements.

Your Requirements	My Qualifications
1. U.S. citizen.	1. Naturalized U.S. Citizen.
2. Strong journalistic skills.	2. Extensive experience researching, gathering information, preparing stories, and presenting facts clearly and succinctly. Nominated for an Emmy award for "Health Care Scam," a medical fraud report.
3. Professional broadcast voice as evidenced by native fluency.	3. Native fluency in English and Spanish. Pleasant, well-controlled voice with good timing. Excellent pronunciation.
4. Excellent translation adaptation abilities with absolute command and fluency in both English and Spanish.	4. Raised in bilingual household. Dual Spanish/English major in college. Correct English and Spanish usage.

I am interested in the challenge this position presents and would like to meet with you and share my enthusiasm and commitment to support the Spanish-speaking community. I have enclosed the writing/translation examples and sample videotape you requested.

Sincerely,

Maria Santiago

Enclosures

> **Television**
> **REPORTER**
> **Spanish Language**
> CABLE USA seeks an experienced TV news reporter/translator for its Spanish-language TV news service located in New York City. The candidate must be a U.S. citizen or permanent resident, possess strong journalistic skills, and have a professional broadcast voice as evidenced by (1) native fluency in Spanish with an acceptable neutral accent for a Latin American TV audience and (2) excellent translation/adaptation abilities with absolute command and fluency in both English and Spanish.
>
> Please send a resume and nonreturnable writing/translation samples and sample videotape to:
> CABLE USA
> 45 Fourth Avenue
> NYC 10021
> Attn: Harriet Wilson

Exhibit 16.

46 Highland Road
San Mateo, California 94400
(415) 377-XXXX

January 11, 1994

Superior Travel, Ltd.
200 Alhambra Street
Carmichael, CA 95608

Dear Ms. Johnson:

Tom Tilden has spoken highly of your organization and recommended I contact you concerning employment possibilities. His enthusiasm is contagious. I would love to be part of a small, customer-oriented organization that provides superior service.

Highlights of my background and achievements, as outlined in the enclosed résumé, include:

• Four years' experience as a Travel Consultant handling international computer reservations and itineraries
• Two years' experience generating and servicing corporate accounts
• Expertise with the Sabre and Cobra computer systems
• Fluent Spanish and French and a working knowledge of Italian

My strongest assets are my interpersonal skills and my love of working with people to make their travel experiences pleasurable.

I'd like to meet with you to learn more about your plans and discuss how I can support your future goals. I'll call to schedule an appointment.

I'll speak with you soon.

Sincerely yours,

Michael Maori

Encl.

Exhibit 17.

---

82 South Main Street
Phoenix, Arizona 85100
(602) 477-XXXX

February 14, 1994

Mr. Ron Meillo
Phoenix Country Day School
Arrowhead Lane
Phoenix, AZ 85007

Dear Mr. Meillo:

Fred Cash recommended that I contact you concerning the opening in your mathematics department. A sound academic background and my dedication to the field of mathematics make me confident I would be a productive addition to your staff.

My qualifications include:

- Fifteen years of experience as a secondary education mathematics educator
- Development, evaluation, and redefinition of math curriculum
- M.Ed. in secondary education and mathematics
- Active participation in the National Council of Teachers of Mathematics

I am committed both to my students and to the field of mathematics. My greatest pleasure is encouraging my students and watching their progress.

I'd welcome the opportunity to meet with you in person to share our goals and discuss how I can support your program.

Yours truly,

Marsha Monk

Encl.

Exhibit 18.

---

89 Wild Way
Orlando, FL 32802

June 30, 1993

Millie Miller, CPA
American Automobile Association
Parkwood Drive
Orlando, FL 32802

Dear Ms. Miller:

Henry Cole suggested that I contact you concerning the Auditor position you advertised for in the June 28, 1993, <u>Orlando Sentinel.</u>

I have four years' experience as an Auditor for the City of Orlando, where I plan and perform effective operational, compliance, program, and financial audits.

My strong analytical, interpersonal, and communication skills have enabled me to gain expertise in developing audit findings and writing and editing audit reports.

The Auditor position is in line with my career goals, as outlined in the enclosed résumé. I would like to meet with you to discuss how my qualifications can meet your needs. I can be reached at (305) 666-XXXX.

Thank you for your consideration.

Yours truly,

Thelma Little, CIA

Encl.

Exhibit 19.

Contact: Julianna White
(805) 999-XXXX

FOR IMMEDIATE RELEASE

MARKETING SPECIALIST SEEKS NEW OPPORTUNITY

Are you in need of a talented professional to write and produce promotional materials, including direct mail, press releases, product sheets, and other marketing and sales support
materials?

If so, Julianna White offers ten years' experience writing and
producing marketing and sales materials that get results. Her
excellent interpersonal and communication skills have enabled
her to work effectively with Product, Sales, and Marketing
Managers, identifying and interpreting their promotional
needs.

Expertise and Accomplishments:
- Ability to plan, coordinate, and produce news releases,
  printed materials, and advertising for an international
  leader in electronic publishing and CD-ROM.
- Experience in developing booth materials and producing
  slides and product announcements for national and international trade shows and related workshops.
- Bachelor of Science in Marketing and desktop publishing
  skills using Pagemaker and Corel Draw.

Julianna is presently employed, but she is available for interviews. For further information call (805) 999-XXXX.

# # #

Exhibit 20.

Russell Mueler

7 Western Way, Phoenix, Arizona 85014 (602) 222-XXXX

February 20, 1993

Golden Development Company
Wade Preston
President
96 Mountain Way
Colorado Springs, CO 80903

Dear Mr. Preston:

If your organization could benefit from creating new business opportunities and improving/expanding existing operations, I think you will find my qualifications to be of interest.

As a senior executive with extensive management experience in design, construction, and operations, I am a recognized specialist in delivering large, complex commercial development programs on time and within budget.

My qualifications are strongest in providing a full range of development-related services for small- to super-regional-size projects, including site planning, engineering, design, construction, and tenant administration. I also contribute expertise and recommendations from land acquisition and predevelopment through design, construction, and property management support.

I currently direct an organization that meets unique client needs by customizing services in project analysis, design management, construction consulting, and tenant coordination for offices, shopping centers, and department stores.

I am interested in taking on a new challenge and would like to discuss opportunities with your organization. I will be in Colorado Springs the week of March 3rd and will call you to set up an appointment.

Thank you for your time.

Sincerely,

Russell Mueler

Exhibit 21.

MARTIN O'RILEY

1244 North 32nd Street, Arlington, Virginia 22204 (703) 522-XXXX

June 1, 1993

National Association of Certified Pharmacists
Ms. Anna Horton
2455 Pennsylvania Avenue
Washington, D.C. 20001

Dear Ms. Horton:

The desire for professional growth sparked my interest in the Executive Director position with your association.

As a resourceful manager with progressive experience and consistent top performance, I am presently Executive Director of a national association. I manage all association operations while promoting and providing annual nationwide competency testing of over 6,000 candidates.

Currently, I work effectively with the Board of Directors, setting agendas for board meetings and preparing annual budgets of $4.6 million. In addition, I oversee development and approval of continuing education and liaison with licensing boards.

My accomplishments include:
- Increasing exam registrations by 141%
- Enhancing association image from national and individual's perspective
- Improving procedures and increased rate of association renewals
- Establishing procedures that resolved paper and computer record problems leading to efficient operations
- Motivating staff to higher productivity while maintaining low turnover rate
- Designing grant procedures and achieving more effective disbursement of funds

My education and credentials include:
- Master's of Science in Public Administration
- Certified Association Executive (C.A.E.) from the American Society of Association Executives

I am confident I can be a valuable addition to your association. I would like to meet with you and discuss how I can assist your association in meeting its goals.

Sincerely,

Martin O'Riley

Part Two
Before and After: Twenty-Five Cover Letter Makeovers

What follows are twenty-five cover letters transformed from passable to powerful. By using these before and after examples you'll see how easy it is to combine effective writing with basic layout skills to create a winning cover letter.

Many of these cover letters are actual samples from clients or workshop participants with whom I have worked. The real names and facts have been changed to protect their privacy.

An original cover letter is presented for each example. Next, comments are provided to pinpoint areas where it might be improved. Finally, a revised cover letter is introduced, implementing the recommendations.

Before we begin I'd just like to offer these few last points about writing a cover letter:

- Make it simple.
- Be direct.
- Keep it uncluttered.
- Be sure to let it reflect your personality.

January 5, 1994

Eastman Kodak
Kodak Park
Rochester, NY 14611

Dear Sir:

Recently, I experienced a change in my career circumstances as a result of my company filing Chapter 11, and the subsequent loss of 5,000 positions. Regretfully, because of short tenure, I was among the casualties.

The objective of this letter is to request your assistance and any possible suggestions you might have in my pursuit of a new position.

I am a team player with a winning attitude, and possess a demonstrated ability to manage multiple projects simultaneously in changing human resources and business environments. Having saved millions of dollars for my employers, I have a seasoned sense and appreciation for the impact of human resources on the "bottom line."

As you will note from the enclosed résumé, I present a results-oriented track record in managing human resources functions. The depth and breadth of my expertise cover the entire spectrum of human resources management inclusive of:

> . Employee/Labor Relations
> . Benefits/Compensation
> . Staffing & Downsizing
> . Affirmative Action
> . Training & Development
> . Total Quality Management Process

I realize my background may not be congruent with your current needs in human resources. However, you may be able to refer me to an organization that can benefit from my expertise. If so, I would appreciate any assistance that you can provide to me. I can be contacted at (716) 888-XXXX.

Your time and consideration are most appreciated. Thank you.

Sincerely,

A. A. Oliver

Encl.

January 5, 1994

Eastman Kodak
Kodak Park
Rochester, NY 14611

Dear Sir:　　　　　　　①

Recently, I experienced a change in my career circumstances as a result of my
company filing Chapter 11, and the subsequent loss of 5,000 positions. Regretfully, because of short tenure, I was among the casualties.

The objective of this letter is to request your assistance and any possible
suggestions you might have in my pursuit of a new position.　②

I am a team player with a winning attitude, and possess a demonstrated ability⎫
to manage multiple projects simultaneously in changing human resources and⎬ ③
business environments. Having saved millions of dollars for my employers, I⎭
have a seasoned sense and appreciation for the impact of human resources on the
"bottom line."

As you will note from the enclosed résumé, I present a results-oriented track
record in managing human resources functions. The depth and breadth of my expertise cover the entire spectrum of human resources management inclusive of:

④ {
. Employee/Labor Relations
. Benefits/Compensation
. Staffing & Downsizing
. Affirmative Action
. Training & Development
. Total Quality Management Process

⑤ I realize my background may not be congruent with your current needs in human
resources. However, you may be able to <u>refer me to</u> an organization that can ⑥
benefit from my expertise. If so, I would appreciate any assistance that you
can provide to me. I can be contacted at (716) 888-XXXX.

Your time and consideration are most appreciated. Thank you.

Sincerely,

A. A. Oliver

Encl.

1. This paragraph is a real downer and will immediately turn off the reader.
2. The objective shouldn't be so blunt. What can you offer the employer?
3. This is good and should be highlighted, not hidden.
4. These are the experiences all human resources managers should have, and it's a waste of space to list them.
5. Weak.
6. Why would someone bother? People don't go to bat for someone they don't know.

Comments

This letter begins on a negative note. You've lost him before you've started. The letter is too long and fails to demonstrate what you can offer.

755 Main Street, Rochester, NY 14617
(716) 888-XXXX

January 5, 1994

Eastman Kodak
Harry Hill
Vice President Administration
Kodak Park
Rochester, NY 14611

Dear Mr. Hill:

As organizations strive to improve productivity and profitability, there is a growing need for human resources professionals who can manage change and transition while appreciating the bottom line.

As a results-oriented team player, I have successfully managed multiple projects simultaneously for changing human resources and business environments in diverse industries.

My experience and accomplishments include:

- Saving thousands of dollars for my employers by designing, implementing, and administering effective personnel/benefits programs
- Successfully establishing nontraditional recruiting methods
- Implementing automated human resources systems (HRIS) for organizational strategic planning and budgetary purposes
- Creating effective relocation and incentive programs
- Preparing EEO/AAP to withstand audits and compliance reviews
- Designing, developing, and producing effective personnel policies and procedures

My career goal is to utilize my human resources expertise in a corporate setting. I would welcome the opportunity to discuss how I can make a contribution to Eastman Kodak. I will call you to set up an appointment.

Sincerely,

A. A. Oliver

Encl.

Before

February 5, 1994

Wildlife Preservation
Dean Jones
P. O. Box 12
The Woodlands, TX 77380

Dear Mr. Jones:

I'm writing to apply for the position of Administrative Assistant to the Communications Manager.

I was made aware of the opening on the posting board at the Texas Employment Commission. I was interested in inquiring further and read the commission's extensive file on your organization. The following information stood out--growth, challenge, teamwork ... the very things I am looking for in a company. That your goal is preservation is above all of great importance to me.

In going over the employment requirements, I am happy to say I do qualify. All of my jobs have included administrative and secretarial responsibilities. I set priorities, follow through to completion, and work well under pressure. I am also detail-oriented. My secretarial skills, including word processing, correspondence handling, record keeping, and effective command of the English language, I believe, also qualify me for this position. Communicating well with the public and all staff levels is my strongest attribute. And, my commitment to preservation is long-standing.

My interest in wildlife goes back to childhood and is kept alive by weekly nature walks. In reading through the Commission's file on your organization, I was impressed by your stand on preservation of natural areas. It is in line with my beliefs about preserving our natural areas.

I want to be part of your team at Wildlife Preservation and aid in preserving our nation's biological environment.

Thank you so much for your consideration.

Very truly yours,

Arthur Green

Enclosure

February 5, 1994

Wildlife Preservation
Dean Jones
P. O. Box 12
The Woodlands, TX 77380

Dear Mr. Jones: ①

I'm writing to apply for the position of Administrative Assistant to the Communications Manager.
                                                    ②
I was made aware of the opening on the posting board at the Texas Employment
Commission. I was interested in inquiring further and read the commission's
extensive file on your organization. The following information stood out--   ③
growth, challenge, teamwork ... the very things I am looking for in a company.
That your goal is preservation is above all of great importance to me.

④

                                                                        ⑤
In going over the employment requirements, I am happy to say I do qualify. All
of my jobs have included administrative and secretarial responsibilities. I
set priorities, follow through to completion, and work well under pressure. I
am also detail-oriented. My secretarial skills, including word processing,
correspondence handling, record keeping, and effective command of the English
language, I believe, also qualify me for this position. Communicating well with
the public and all staff levels is my strongest attribute. And, my commitment
to preservation is long-standing.

My interest in wildlife goes back to childhood and is kept alive by weekly ⑥
nature walks. In reading through the Commission's file on your organization,
I was impressed by your stand on preservation of natural areas. It is in line
with my beliefs about preserving our natural areas.

I want to be part of your team at Wildlife Preservation and aid in preserving
our nation's biological environment.

Thank you so much for your consideration.

                              Very truly yours,

                              Arthur Green

Enclosure

1. It's obvious you're writing. Draft a more effective, catchy beginning.
2. Do you need to mention the posting board? Determine the relevance of all information prior to including it.
3. Good beginning, but build on it and strengthen.
4. Awkward. This isn't correct sentence structure.
5. Awkward. State how you qualify.
6. This is good. Expand and make it stronger.

Comments
Long and awkwardly constructed. Build on the nature interest and personalize. It will have a uniqueness all its own.

7553 Broadway
Houston, TX 77050
(713) 733-XXXX

February 5, 1994

Wildlife Preservation
Dean Jones
P. O. Box 12
The Woodlands, TX 77380

Dear Mr. Jones:

    Your job announcement for an Administrative Assistant to the Communications Manager intrigued me. I did some research and discovered that Wildlife Preservation offers growth, challenge, and teamwork, the very things I'm looking for in an organization. Your mission in preservation added to my excitement and desire to be a member of your organization.

    My seven years of secretarial and administrative experience qualify me for the position. I possess excellent communication skills and the ability to work well with all staff levels. I am able to set priorities and follow assignments through to completion. In addition, I hold a life-long commitment to preservation.

    Nature has played an integral part in my life since childhood and has kindled a passionate fascination for plants and wildlife. My interest in your organization was piqued by your articles on Big Thicket Natural Preserve and Alabama-Coushatta Indian Reservation. While living in Beaumont, Texas, I had the opportunity to navigate the Village Creek and experience the fauna and flora.

    I want to be part of your team at Wilderness Preservation and help safeguard our nation's biological heritage. I look forward to speaking with you and exploring your needs and my qualifications in more detail.

                              Sincerely yours,

                              Arthur Green

Enclosure

March 1, 1994

National Foods
22 Sandstone Road
Eau Claire, WI 54700

Dear Sir/Madam:

In the event that there may be a mutually beneficial position open, I have
enclosed a copy of my résumé.

For the past five years, I have worked for a large school system, establishing
and coordinating a computer lab. I have developed an expertise in training
students and adults in utilizing computer software.

My goal is to transfer these experiences to a corporate environment, developing
programs and training individuals on computer applications.

I will appreciate the opportunity to discuss my qualifications at your convenience. I can be reached at (715) 777-XXXX.

Yours truly,

Jack Flood

Enc.

March 1, 1994

National Foods
22 Sandstone Road
Eau Claire, WI 54700

Dear Sir/Madam: ①   ②

In the event that there may be a mutually beneficial position open, I have enclosed a copy of my résumé.

For the past five years, I have worked for a large school system, establishing and coordinating a computer lab. I have developed an expertise in training ③
students and adults in utilizing computer software.

④ My goal is to transfer these experiences to a corporate environment, developing programs and training individuals on computer applications.
   ⑤
I will appreciate the opportunity to discuss my qualifications at your convenience. I can be reached at (715) 777-XXXX.
              ⑥
Yours truly,

Jack Flood

Enc.

Comments

1. Direct the letter to a specific individual.
2. Too vague. An opening like this will be dismissed. You must indicate what position you're interested in.
3. These are both good selling points and should be highlighted.
4. This is the purpose of your letter. Place it at the beginning instead of the end of your letter.
5. Use a more positive, assertive close.
6. You won't get a phone call from an unsolicited letter. You need to call them.

Comments

Unsolicited letters need to attract attention immediately. Clearly state what you have to offer and, if possible, that you can fill a need.

63 Fall Street
Eau Claire, WI 54704
(715) 777-XXXX

March 1, 1994

National Foods
Ms. Fitzgerald
Director of Training
22 Sandstone Road
Eau Claire, WI 54700

Dear Ms. Fitzgerald:

   Are your employees effectively using their computer software? According to a new study conducted by PC Users magazine, 73% of all employees learn only the basics of computer software.

   Let me increase your employees' productivity by designing and conducting training programs for groups and individuals so that they can use their software efficiently.

   For the past five years, I have worked for a large school system, where I established and coordinated a computer lab and developed computer software courses and curricula to satisfy student needs.

   My expertise in computer applications resulted in my designation as the "PC Expert" for the entire school system. Now I would like to put my experience and skills to use at National Foods as a technical trainer.

   The enclosed résumé provides more information on my background. I'd like to meet with you to discuss your organizational needs, and I will call you to schedule an appointment.

   Thank you for your time.

                              Yours truly,

                              Jack Flood

Encl.

October 3, 1993

Pepperdine University
Ms. Sally Street
Dean of Students
12 Beach Lane
Malibu, CA 90265

Dear Dean Street:

I have recently learned of the opening at Pepperdine University for the position of Assistant Dean of Students. Enclosed is my résumé for your review.

I am currently employed at a large university. After one year, I find it does not present the challenge or opportunities I seek. Therefore, I have decided to seek a new position.

As my résumé indicates, I have had extensive supervisory responsibility as a professional hall director and provided systemwide training to both graduate and undergraduate staff. In addition, I have been charged with the selection, training, and evaluation of 30 students and faculty members in my capacity as Director of New Student Orientation and Adjudication at California Polytechnic State University.

I feel that my skills as a student affairs generalist make me well equipped to function as the Assistant Dean of Students. I feel that my career interests would prove compatible with the goals of your student affairs program and would enable me to assist in developing the leadership potential of the students at Pepperdine.

I feel I have the energy, skills, and creativity to make a valuable contribution to Pepperdine and I would welcome the opportunity to meet with you to discuss my candidacy. I can be reached at (805) 666-XXXX. I look forward to further correspondence with you.

Sincerely,

Tom Fox

encl.

October 3, 1993

Pepperdine University
Ms. Sally Street
Dean of Students
12 Beach Lane
Malibu, CA 90265

Dear Dean Street:

①
 I have recently learned of the opening at Pepperdine University for the position of Assistant Dean of Students. Enclosed is my résumé for your review.

 I am currently employed at a large university. After one year, I find it ②
does not present the challenge or opportunities I seek. Therefore, I have decided to seek a new position.

④
 As my résumé indicates, I have had extensive supervisory responsibility as a professional hall director and provided systemwide training to both graduate and undergraduate staff. In addition, I have been charged with the <u>selection,</u> ③
<u>training, and evaluation</u> of 30 students and faculty members in my capacity as Director of New Student Orientation and Adjudication at California Polytechnic State University.

⑤
 <u>I feel</u> that my skills as a student affairs generalist make me well equipped to function as the Assistant Dean of Students. <u>I feel</u> that my career interests would prove compatible with the goals of your student affairs program and would enable me to assist in developing the leadership potential of the students at Pepperdine.

 <u>I feel</u> I have the <u>energy, skills, and creativity to make a valuable con-</u> ⑥
<u>tribution</u> to Pepperdine and I would welcome the opportunity to meet with you to discuss my candidacy. I can be reached at (805) 666-XXXX. I look forward to further correspondence with you. ⑦

Sincerely,

Tom Fox

encl.

Comments

1. Avoid *I*. Begin with something more striking.
2. This is weak. What experience do you have to offer?
3. Rewrite in the same grammatical form.
4. Incorporate the two paragraphs.
5. "I feel" is redundant.
6. This is good, but it should go at the beginning of the letter.
7. The next step in the process is a conversation, not correspondence. "I look forward to speaking with you" is more appropriate.

Comments

There's no doubt the writer is well-qualified. Qualifications and interest should appear at the beginning rather than be led up to at the end.

13 Coral Court
Los Angeles, California 90009
(213) 666-XXXX

October 3, 1993

Pepperdine University
Ms. Sally Street
Dean of Students
12 Beach Lane
Malibu, CA 90265

Dear Dean Street:

I would like the opportunity to put my energy, drive, and enthusiasm to work for you as the Assistant Dean of Students.

Directing a residence hall system the size of the one at Pepperdine seems to be a natural step in my career progression. As my résumé indicates, I have had substantial supervisory responsibility as a professional hall director, in which capacity I have provided systemwide training to both undergraduate and graduate staff. Additionally, I selected, trained, and evaluated 30 students and faculty members as Director of New Student Orientation and Adjudication at California Polytechnic State University.

The training component has given me satisfaction and pleasure in all of my student affairs positions. So much "floor time" has developed my confidence and skills in stand-up training and my ability to market and deliver effective and creative programs.

Most recently, my skills were put to use at a large university, where I designed a residence hall manual, drafted a proposal for a residential judicial system, and planned orientation training for paraprofessional staff.

My career interests are compatible with the goals of your student affairs program and would enable me to assist in developing the leadership potential of the students at Pepperdine.

I would like the opportunity to meet with you and discuss my candidacy. I will call you to schedule an appointment.

Sincerely,

Tom Fox

Encl.

7554 M Street, NW
Washington, D.C. 20001
(202) 433-XXXX

September 1, 1993

Mr. Thomas Toth
National Policy Forum
7 Pennsylvania Avenue
Washington, D.C. 20003

Dear Mr. Toth:

Congratulations on being named President of the National Policy Forum.   I am
pleased to see the Republican Party launch a process to undertake a discussion
of some issues that need clarification.   I've discussed the project with Bill
Smith and Jane Thomas and they praised your efforts and recommended that I get
in touch with you.

I want to become a part of this program.   My experience includes:

   o National political campaigns
   oPublic Relations Director for national organization of
      over 200,000 membership;
              . conducted national survey of membership
              . co-ordinate media events and materials
              . created an award-winning advertising campaign
   o Small business experience;
              . started own company
              . designed computer information system
              . created marketing and advertising material
   o Experienced public speaker
   o Qualified fund raiser

These experiences, plus an enthusiasm for the project, would, I believe, make
me an asset to the project.

I am very interested in meeting with you and discussing how I can contribute
to the project effort.

Sincerely,

Maureen Ruff

Encl.

7554 M Street, NW
Washington, D.C. 20001
(202) 433-XXXX

September 1, 1993

Mr. Thomas Toth
National Policy Forum
7 Pennsylvania Avenue
Washington, D.C. 20003

Dear Mr. Toth:

Congratulations on being named President of the National Policy Forum. I am
pleased to see the Republican Party launch a process to undertake a discussion——①
of some issues that need clarification. I've discussed the project with Bill
Smith and Jane Thomas and they praised your efforts and recommended that I get
in touch with you.

②———I want to become a part of this program. My experience includes:

③
    o National political campaigns
    oPublic Relations Director for national organization of
       over 200,000 membership;
         . conducted national survey of membership
       ④. co-ordinate media events and materials   ⑤
         . created an award-winning advertising campaign
    o Small business experience;
       . started own company
       . designed computer information system
       . created marketing and advertising material
    o Experienced public speaker
    o Qualified fund raiser

⑥—— These experiences, plus an enthusiasm for the project, would, I _believe_, make
me an asset to the project.

I am very interested in meeting with you and discussing how I can contribute
to the project effort.

Sincerely,

Maureen Ruff

Encl.

1. Good idea, but it needs editing and tightening up.
2. Need a better introduction.
3. Align the first letters after the bullets and add some space.
4. Watch out for shift in tenses.
5. Take these points and summarize separately.
6. Be more convincing.

Comments

The letter needs better organization and a more appealing format. Take the experiences that relate to the project, then edit and highlight.

7554 M Street, NW
Washington, D.C. 20001
(202) 433-XXXX

September 1, 1993

Mr. Thomas Toth
National Policy Forum
7 Pennsylvania Avenue
Washington, D.C. 20003

Dear Mr. Toth:

Congratulations on your appointment as President of the National
Policy Forum. I am pleased to see the Republican Party undertake this
mission to clarify high-priority domestic issues. I've discussed the
project with Bill Smith and Jane Thomas, and both of them praised your
efforts and recommended I contact you.

The project excites me, and I would like to be a part of your team.
The scope of my experience, detailed in the enclosed résumé, includes:

* Active participation in national political campaigns
* Position as Public Relations Director for a national organization
  with over 200,000 members
* Establishment and operation of a successful small business; de-
  signed a computer management information system
* Extensive development and implementation of revenue-generating
  fund-raising activities
* Experience as a seasoned, effective public speaker

My public relations qualifications include conducting a national
survey of membership, coordinating media events and materials, developing
marketing and advertising materials, and creating an award-winning advertising program.

I'm available to meet with you to discuss how I can contribute to
the project's success and will call you to schedule an appointment.

Sincerely,

Maureen Ruff

Encl.

April 12, 1993

Harper & Harper
88 Seventh Avenue
St. Louis, MO 63110

Dear Ms. Tree:

I am writing in regard to the accounting position advertised in the <u>Post Dispatch</u> last Sunday.

I come highly recommended as an accountant and can supply letters of recommendation from my supervisors, upon request.

My enclosed résumé highlights my qualifications:

- o Five years of experience with a CPA firm

- o Master's degree in Accounting

- o Expertise in using automated accounting systems.

I am presently employed by a large, local real estate developer as a Tax Accountant. After one year in this position, I find it does not present the challenge or variety I experienced in public accounting. Therefore, I have decided to return to public accounting.

I am seeking an organization which offers a challenging and professional environment as well as growth potential, which does not exist in my present firm.

I look forward to hearing from you so that we can speak about employment opportunities at Harper & Harper.

Truly yours,

Sunny Michaels

Encl.

April 12, 1993

Harper & Harper
88 Seventh Avenue
St. Louis, MO 63110

Dear Ms. Tree: ①

I am writing <u>in regard to</u> the accounting position advertised in the <u>Post Dis-</u>
<u>patch</u> last Sunday.   ②

I <u>come highly recommended</u> as an accountant and <u>can supply letters of recommen-</u>
<u>dation</u> from my supervisors, upon request.

My enclosed résumé highlights my qualifications:

    o Five years of experience with a CPA firm

    o Master's degree in Accounting

    o Expertise in using automated accounting systems.

I am presently employed by a large, local real estate developer as a Tax Ac-   ③
countant. After one year in this position, I find it does not present the
<u>challenge</u> or variety I experienced in public accounting. Therefore, I have
decided to return to public accounting.   ④

I am seeking an organization which offers a <u>challenging</u> and professional environment as well as growth potential, <u>which does not exist</u> in my present firm.
                                                          ⑤
I look forward to hearing from you so that we can speak about employment opportunities at Harper & Harper.

Truly yours,

Sunny Michaels

Encl.

Comments

1. Are you interested? If so, state it here.
2. Organizations want to know what you have to offer, not what someone else will say about you.
3. This sounds negative. Rephrase and make it positive.
4. *Challenge* is redundant. Find another word.
5. This is also negative.

Comments

Emphasize your qualifications, not your dissatisfaction with your current employer.

8900 Edglea Circle
St. Louis, Missouri 63118
(314) 624-XXXX

April 12, 1993

Harper & Harper
88 Seventh Avenue
St. Louis, MO 63110

Dear Ms. Tree:

I was delighted when I saw your advertisement for an Accountant in the April 9th <u>Post Dispatch.</u> I was struck by the similarities in your requirements and my accounting background.

The enclosed résumé highlights my background and achievements:

• Five years of experience with a CPA firm
• Master's degree in Accounting
• Expertise in using automated accounting systems

As a Tax Accountant for a large, local real estate developer, I miss the challenge, intensity, and variety I experienced in public accounting.

The combination of my technical ability, experience, and hardworking nature makes me a viable candidate. I look forward to hearing from you and scheduling an appointment to discuss employment opportunities at Harper & Harper.

Sincerely yours,

Sunny Michaels

Encl.

March 3, 1994

Southern Systems
Personnel Director
2001 Sixth Street
Charlotte, NC 28213

Dear Gentlemen:

Your help wanted ad in the March 1 <u>Observer</u> described your need for a computer programmer. I am very interested, for this could be the challenge I seek and lead to a solid career with you.

My confidence in my education, training, and experience in computer programming is supported by experience on a broad range of systems from PC's to mainframes in an equally broad range of operating environments.

My experience relevant to your requirements includes:

full-cycle application development from needs assessment to systems design, programming, testing, installation, training, and maintenance;

background in secondary and post-secondary education applicable to CBT and cur-riculum development.

experience in course development using TenCORE 2.0;

extensive working knowledge of Macintosh and IBM-PC desktop applications em-phasizing graphics; and

self-starting analytical abilities applied to independent work or team efforts as appropriate.

The enclosed résumé outlines my qualifications for this position. After re-viewing it, please write or call to discuss my qualifications and set up an interview with me.

Sincerely,

Juan Cabrera

enc.

March 3, 1994

Southern Systems
Personnel Director
2001 Sixth Street
Charlotte, NC 28213

Dear Gentlemen: ①

Your help wanted ad in the March 1 <u>Observer</u> described your need for a computer ⎫
programmer. I am very interested, for this could be the challenge I seek and ⎬ ②
lead to a solid career with you. ⎭

③

My <u>confidence</u> in my education, training, and experience in computer programming
is supported by experience on a broad range of systems from PC's to mainframes
in an equally broad range of operating environments.

My experience relevant to your requirements includes:

full-cycle application development from needs assessment to systems design,
programming, testing, installation, training, and maintenance;

background in secondary and post-secondary education applicable to CBT and curriculum development.

④ experience in course development using TenCORE 2.0;

extensive working knowledge of Macintosh and IBM-PC desktop applications em-
phasizing graphics; and

self-starting analytical abilities applied to independent work or team efforts
as appropriate.

The enclosed résumé outlines my qualifications for this position. After re-
viewing it, <u>please write or call</u> to discuss my qualifications and set up an
interview with me.   ⑤

                    Sincerely,

                    Juan Cabrera

enc.

1. If the reader is a woman, she'll be turned off immediately. Try *Dear Employer.*
2. Very self-serving. Employers want to know what you can do for them, not what they can do for you.
3. Weak. Find a better word.
4. Begin each point by capitalizing first word and indenting. End punctuation is incorrect.
5. Bid directly for an interview. Also, how can they call without a phone number?

Comments
Focus on demonstrating your strong qualifications.

17 Rose Hill Court, Charlotte, North Carolina 28210
(704) 922-XXXX

March 3, 1994

Southern Systems
Personnel Director
2001 Sixth Street
Charlotte, NC 28213

Dear Personnel Director:

Are you looking for broad computer and instructional experience in a mid-senior-level professional? If so, I may be the computer programmer you advertised for in the March 1st Observer.

The development of quality CBT systems requires a blend of instructional design experience and a thorough grasp of computer programming techniques. My credentials include the following skills necessary for productivity on your projects:

- Full-cycle application development from needs assessment to systems design, programming, testing, installation, training, and maintenance
- Education and training applicable to CBT and curriculum development
- Experience in course development using TenCORE 2.0
- Extensive working knowledge of Macintosh and IBM-PC desktop applications emphasizing graphics
- Self-starting and analytical abilities applied to independent work or team efforts, as appropriate

The enclosed résumé can't reveal the many details that make the difference between a so-so employee and one who contributes daily. I am ready to meet with you personally to determine if a match exists and then discuss employment possibilities.

Sincerely,

Juan Cabrera

Encl.

May 12, 1993

Chicago Area Rapid Transit
Human Resources
Dept. 667/3111
2990 Main Street
Chicago, IL 60614

Dear Employer:

Your Open Position Notice for the Chief Auditor position really piqued my interest. To give you a brief idea of my background and qualifications, I have enclosed a copy of my résumé.

As my résumé indicates, I have extensive experience in internal audit operations either as director, or staff auditor. I have been responsible for and successful at training, motivating, and directing large staffs and am well respected for my communication and interpersonal relations skills.

I have had some challenging management experience. I was a Director of Internal Audit in the Air Force for four years and during that time acted as consultant and advisor on Fraud, Waste and Abuse matters. I managed a $5 Billion aircraft production budget with all the attendant responsibilities. I was actively involved in fraud investigations and am currently a Certified Fraud Examiner along with being a Certified Internal Auditor.

All modesty aside, I have been highly commended for past endeavors. I am a manager, trainer, communicator!

I am confident that I can serve on your staff in a capacity which will be mutually beneficial, and am eager to talk with you further about my qualifications.

Sincerely,

MARLIN FISHER

Résumé enclosed

May 12, 1993

Chicago Area Rapid Transit
Human Resources
Dept. 667/3111
2990 Main Street
Chicago, IL 60614

Dear Employer:

① Your Open Position Notice for the Chief Auditor position really piqued my interest. To give you a brief idea of my background and qualifications, I have enclosed a copy of my résumé. ②

② As my résumé indicates, I have extensive experience in internal audit opera- ③ tions either as director, or staff auditor. I have been responsible for and successful at training, motivating, and directing large staffs and am well respected for my communication and interpersonal relations skills.

④ I have had some challenging management experience. I was a Director of Internal Audit in the Air Force for four years and during that time acted as consultant ⑤ and advisor on Fraud, Waste and Abuse matters. I managed a $5 Billion aircraft production budget with all the attendant responsibilities. I was actively involved in fraud investigations and am currently a Certified Fraud Examiner along with being a Certified Internal Auditor.

⑥ All modesty aside, I have been highly commended for past endeavors. I am a manager, trainer, communicator!

I am confident that I can serve on your staff in a capacity which will be mutually beneficial, and am eager to talk with you further about my qualifications.

Sincerely,

MARLIN FISHER
                    ⑦
Résumé enclosed

1. Why did it pique your interest? This is where you need to catch attention.
2. You don't need to mention your résumé twice.
3. This is stated awkwardly.
4. Too many *I*'s.
5. These are all good points. Split them out.
6. This sounds too much like bragging. If you want to use a statement like this, quote someone else's assessment of your performance from either your appraisal or a letter of commendation.
7. Your name should not appear in all caps.

Comments

Letters must highlight qualifications, not hide them. List those of your qualifications that meet the job requirements, and make them clearly visible in your organization and format.

47 Park Street
Chicago, Illinois 60610
(312) 621-XXXX

May 12, 1993

Chicago Area Rapid Transit
Ms. Katherine Chubb
Director of Recruitment
Dept. 667/3111
2990 Main Street
Chicago, IL 60614

Dear Ms. Chubb:

The open position notice for the Chief Auditor is an exact match between your job requirements and my qualifications.

My background includes extensive internal audit operations experience in successfully directing, training, and motivating large staffs.

Selected experience and skills include:

• Four years as Director of Internal Audit, Air Force; consulted and advised on fraud, waste, and abuse matters; managed a $5 billion aircraft production budget.
• Extensive experience in fraud investigations.
• Excellent communication and interpersonal skills.
• Certified Fraud Examiner and Certified Internal Auditor.
• Recipient of superior performance commendations for audit management.

I am interested in joining your staff and am eager to speak with you and discuss how I can support your audit program.

Sincerely,

Marlin Fisher

Enclosure

Before

March 3, 1994

Central Investment Corp.
33 Park Avenue
New York, NY 10020

Dear Mr. Burns:

Your organization is one which I have selected to contact following some careful research into such considerations as location, markets, and other related business factors. I am currently seeking an opportunity to excel in a dynamic company as well as have the opportunity to utilize my educational background.

I will graduate in June from the Wharton School of Business and plan to pursue a career in real estate. I understand that your office is presently trying to fill an Assistant Project Manager position. I am interested in applying for this position.

I have enclosed a copy of my résumé for your review. My professional career exhibits a record of strong achievements and significant contributions.

I would welcome the opportunity to discuss my qualifications and your needs. I can be reached at (215) 555-4444.

Sincerely,

Barry Meade

enc.

March 3, 1994

Central Investment Corp.
33 Park·Avenue
New York, NY 10020

Dear Mr. Burns:

①

Your organization is one which I have selected to contact following some careful
research into such considerations as location, markets, and other related business factors. I am currently seeking an opportunity to excel in a dynamic company as well as have the opportunity to utilize my educational background. } ②

③ { I will graduate in June from the Wharton School of Business and plan to pursue
a career in real estate. I understand that your office is presently trying to
fill an Assistant Project Manager position. I am interested in applying for
this position.

I have enclosed a copy of my résumé for your review. My professional career
exhibits a record of strong achievements and significant contributions. } ④

I would welcome the opportunity to discuss my qualifications and your needs.
I can be reached at (215) 555-4444. ⑤

Sincerely,

Barry Meade

enc.

1. Good ideas but poor beginning. Develop them in the second paragraph.
2. Self-serving. What can *you* offer?
3. This is the purpose of your letter and should be in the first paragraph.
4. What are your achievements and contributions?
5. It's up to you to initiate contact.

Comments
There are good ideas in the first paragraph. Use them in the second paragraph and build on them.

87 Third Avenue
New York, NY 10002
(212) 655-XXXX

March 3, 1994

Central Investment Corp.
33 Park Avenue
New York, NY 10020

Dear Mr. Burns:

I will graduate from the Wharton School of Business in June and plan to pursue a career in real estate.

Your firm interests me, and I have kept abreast of its activities through industry contacts, articles in the press, and a campus presentation made by Bill Hamilton and Sarah James of your Philadelphia office. I've learned through my research of your firm's continuing ability to realize successful development projects while establishing and maintaining relationships with sources of capital — and I'm impressed.

I understand that your office is presently seeking an Assistant Project Manager. I am interested in applying for this position and request the opportunity to speak with you or one of your associates in the next few weeks.

I have enclosed a copy of my résumé for your review. You will find me bright, highly motivated, eager to take on responsibility, and in possession of developed real estate analytical skills.

Thank you for your consideration. I will contact you next week to gain a better sense of what your needs may be.

Sincerely,

Barry Meade

Encl.

September 4, 1993

Dear Sir:

Please find enclosed a copy of my résumé for your consideration. I am interested in applying for the position of Director of Administration you advertised in the September 3, 1993, <u>Boston Globe.</u>

The enclosed résumé reflects my solid qualifications for this position. I hold a Masters in Business Administration from Boston College. In addition, my work history includes experience as a Personnel Manager with overall responsibility in personnel administration. In this position, I developed personnel policies, negotiated employment contracts, and administered compensation programs.

While lacking hands-on experience, most recently, I have attended workshops on proposal development and plan on developing this skill.

I believe my education and experience would enable me to contribute effectively to this position. Please contact me to discuss my background further, if my qualifications meet your organization's needs.

Thank you for your time and consideration.

Truly yours,

Sam Copley

encl.

Management
  DIRECTOR ADMINISTRATION

Medium-size international development firm seeks a mid-career administrator to manage its companywide support services.

Candidates must possess the following skills and experience:

* Master's degree in management, finance, or administrative sciences
* Demonstrated hands-on experience in automated office systems
* Background in human resources and personnel administration, including
  policies, employment contracts, and compensation
* Proposal development and coordination

To be considered, please send a resumé by September 9 to Box 4555, Boston, MA 02215

September 4, 1993

① Dear Sir:

② Please find enclosed a copy of my résumé for your consideration. I am interested in applying for the position of Director of Administration you advertised in the September 3, 1993, Boston Globe.

The enclosed résumé reflects my solid qualifications for this position. I hold a Masters in Business Administration from Boston College. In addition, my work history includes experience as a Personnel Manager with overall responsibility in personnel administration. In this position, I developed personnel policies, negotiated employment contracts, and administered compensation programs. ③

④ While lacking hands-on experience, most recently, I have attended workshops on proposal development and plan on developing this skill.

I believe my education and experience would enable me to contribute effectively to this position. Please contact me to discuss my background further, if my qualifications meet your organization's needs.

⑤ Thank you for your time and consideration.

Truly yours,

Sam Copley

encl.

Management
DIRECTOR ADMINISTRATION

Medium-size international development firm seeks a mid-career administrator to manage its companywide support services.

Candidates must possess the following skills and experience:

* Master's degree in management, finance, or administrative sciences
* Demonstrated hands-on experience in automated office systems
* Background in human resources and personnel administration, including policies, employment contracts, and compensation
* Proposal development and coordination

To be considered, please send a resumé by September 9 to Box 4555, Boston, MA 02215

1. Inside address and phone number missing.
2. Weak introduction.
3. This is a reiteration of the ad and needs more depth.
4. This is negative. Rephrase and use the training as a positive.
5. This leaves some doubt as to your qualifications. Be more positive in assuming your qualifications *do* meet their needs.

Comments
Demonstrate that your qualifications match the job requirements. Be positive!

900 Harris Lane, Boston, MA 02110
(617) 322-XXXX

September 4, 1993

Search Committee
Director Administration Position
Box 4555
Boston, MA 02215

Dear Search Committee:

   I am confident my background makes me a viable candidate for the Director of Administration position advertised in the September 3rd Boston
Globe.

   The following highlights how my experience and accomplishments meet
your qualifications.

YOU REQUIRE:	I HAVE:
Master's degree in Management.	Master's degree in Business Administration from Boston College.
Demonstrated hands-on experience in automated systems.	Experience in utilizing and recommending enhancements to automated human resources system.
Background in human resources and personnel administration, including policies, employment contracts, and compensation.	Ten years' experience in personnel administration, five years as a Personnel Manager. Expertise in developing personnel policies, negotiating employment contracts, and administering compensation programs.
Proposal development and coordination.	Completion of two workshops: "Writing Effective Proposals" and "Proposal Management."

The enclosed résumé provides more detailed information on my background.
I would like the opportunity to meet with you in person to discuss your
needs and how I can meet them. I look forward to speaking with you.

Sincerely,

Sam Copley

Encl.

12 Hollywood Avenue
Tuckahoe, NY 10707

May 13, 1993

Mr. William Ralston
Personnel Director
Prestigious Plants
66 Post Road
Eastchester, NY 10709

Dear Mr. Ralston:

My strong work ethic and my horticultural ability are already developed, areas
that I feel will be of value to your organization.

I will graduate from Westchester Community College in June with an Associate's
in Applied Science in Landscape Design.

I would like to put my skills and training to work at Prestigious Plants. We
should get together and discuss how I can be of help to you.

                    Sincerely,

                    Jessie White

enc.

12 Hollywood Avenue
Tuckahoe, NY 10707

May 13, 1993

Mr. William Ralston
Personnel Director
Prestigious Plants
66 Post Road
Eastchester, NY 10709

Dear Mr. Ralston:

My strong work ethic and my horticultural ability are already developed, areas ②
that I feel will be of value to your organization.

I will graduate from Westchester Community College in June with an Associate's
in Applied Science in Landscape Design.

I would like to put my <u>skills and training</u> to work at Prestigious Plants. We
should get together and discuss how I can be of help to you. ④

Sincerely,

Jessie White

enc.

1. Odd statement.
2. Reorganize and reword the introduction. This is an unsolicited letter, so you need to grab attention.
3. Elaborate on your skills and training.
4. You need to offer them information that makes them want to get together with you.

Comments

Unsolicited letters must have personality—that is, they must be catchy and appealing. You need to showcase what you've got to offer. Your letter must make an impression and trigger a desire to meet you.

12 Hollywood Avenue
Tuckahoe, NY 10707
(914) 611-XXXX

May 13, 1993

Mr. William Ralston
Personnel Director
Prestigious Plants
66 Post Road
Eastchester, NY 10709

Dear Mr. Ralston:

My family claims I was born with a green thumb! An early interest in and knack with plants nurtured a desire in me to pursue a career in horticulture.

I will graduate from Westchester Community College in June with an Associate's degree in Applied Science and a major in Landscape Design.

While my abilities and training are a plus, I am also a dedicated hard worker who doesn't mind starting at the ground floor and working my way up.

I would like to meet with you and discuss how I can contribute to your organization while making my career dreams a reality. I will call you to set up an appointment.

Sincerely yours,

Jessie White

Enc.

February 19, 1994

Bank of Seattle
Attn: Human Resources Division
78 Oceanside
Seattle, WA 98104

Dear Human Resources Division:

I have enclosed a copy of my résumé for your consideration for the Data Processing Supervisor position you advertised in the February 16 <u>Seattle Post-
Intelligencer.</u>

I think you'll find the following credentials parallel your requirements:

   o Bachelor of Science in Information Systems
   o Two years' experience on an IBM 3090 mainframe
   o LAN administrator for a 30-server Token Ring network
      running under Novell Netware
   o Perform all software and hardware maintenance

Thank you for your consideration. I look forward to hearing from you soon and
setting up an acceptable interview time to further discuss my qualifications.

Sincerely yours,

Paula Gillis

Enclosure

February 19, 1994

Bank of Seattle
Attn: Human Resources Division
78 Oceanside
Seattle, WA 98104

Dear Human Resources Division: ①

I have enclosed a copy of my résumé for your ② consideration for the Data Processing Supervisor position you advertised in the February 16 <u>Seattle Post-
Intelligencer.</u>

③

I <u>think you'll find</u> the following credentials parallel your requirements:

    o Bachelor of Science in Information Systems
    o Two years' experience on an IBM 3090 mainframe
    o LAN administrator for a 30-server Token Ring network
       running under Novell Netware
⑤——o Perform all software and hardware maintenance

④

⑥

Thank you for your consideration. I look forward to hearing from you soon and
<u>setting up an acceptable</u> interview time to further discuss my qualifications.

Sincerely yours, ⑦

Paula Gillis

Enclosure

1. Try *Director.*
2. You're qualified—why not state it in the opening paragraph?
3. If you're uncertain, they surely will be! Use a stronger statement.
4. Add some technical qualifications.
5. Is this really important?
6. Create a stronger close.
7. For whom? This sounds awkward. You'll make yourself available for an interview, so state it that way.

Comments

The tone of your letter needs to be more confident. Be specific and focus on the qualifications that meet the job requirements.

556 Harpkins Lane
Seattle, WA 98100
(206) 422-XXXX

February 19, 1994

Bank of Seattle
Attn: Human Resources Division
78 Oceanside
Seattle, WA 98104

Dear Human Resources Director:

My extensive computer and PC experience qualifies me for the Data Processing Supervisor position advertised in the February 16 <u>Seattle Post-
Intelligencer.</u>

The following credentials, as detailed in the enclosed résumé, match your
requirements:

- Bachelor of Science in Information Systems
- Two years of supervisory experience managing operations in an IBM
  3090 mainframe environment
- Knowledgeable in both VM and MVS operating systems
- Considerable experience as a LAN administrator for a 30-server To-
  ken Ring network running under Novell Netware
- Proficient in DOS (Windows), O/S 2, and UNIX operating systems

If you are looking for someone with strong technical skills and a will-
ingness to work hard to get the job done, please contact me to schedule a
meeting.

I look forward to hearing from you.

                        Sincerely yours,

                        Paula Gillis

Enclosure

November 17, 1993

Baker Products
38 Hemming Way
Lansing, MI 48921

Dear Employer:

I am interested in applying for the position of Credit and Collection Manager as advertised in the November 14, 1993, addition of the <u>Detroit Free Press.</u> I have the required qualifications and am confident your operation can provide an excellent vehicle to expand on my skills.

As the enclosed résumé indicates, I am an enthusiastic and dedicated manager with extensive experience in credit and collections.

I have excellent management skills and have created training programs to motivate my staff to consistently exceed corporate targets.

As outlined in the enclosed résumé, I have six years' experience developing and implementing credit and collection programs and maintaining cash flows for $55 million in annual revenue.

Sincerely,

Jonathan Riley

Encl.

Before and After

November 17, 1993

Baker Products
38 Hemming Way
Lansing, MI 48921

Dear Employer:

I am interested in applying for the position of Credit and Collection Manager
as advertised in the November 14, 1993, <u>addition</u> of the <u>Detroit Free Press.</u> I ①
have the required qualifications and am confident your operation can provide ②
an excellent vehicle to expand on my skills.

As the <u>enclosed résumé</u> indicates, I am an enthusiastic and dedicated manager ③
with extensive experience in credit and collections.

④ { I have excellent management skills and have created training programs to motivate my staff to consistently exceed corporate targets.

⑤
As outlined in the <u>enclosed résumé,</u> I have six years' experience developing and ⎫
implementing credit and collection programs and maintaining cash flows for $55 ⎬ ⑥
million in annual revenue.   ⎭

Sincerely,   ⑦

Jonathan Riley

Encl.

1. This word is both incorrectly spelled (should be *edition*) and unnecessary.
2. This is self-serving. Explain why *they* should be interested in you.
3. How can a resumé indicate enthusiasm?
4. This is good; develop it.
5. Redundant.
6. Your experience should be of interest to the employer. Use it at the beginning instead of the end.
7. What about a close?

Comments

Letter fails to show why an employer should be interested.

82 Whisper Lane
Lansing, Michigan 48920
(517) 724-XXXX

November 17, 1993

Baker Products
38 Hemming Way
Lansing, MI 48921

Dear Employer:

My extensive experience in credit and collections suggests that I may be
the Credit and Collections Manager you seek as advertised in the November
14 Detroit Free Press.

As outlined in the enclosed résumé, I have six years' experience developing and implementing credit and collection programs and maintaining
cash flows for $55 million in annual revenue.

Selected Experience and Accomplishments Include:

- Expertise in handling all aspects of industrial credit evaluation
- Outstanding performance results; consistently exceeding corporate
  collection targets
- Highly motivated and effective manager; skillfully train and guide
  staff of seven Credit and Collection Specialists, reducing turnover
  and increasing job satisfaction

My strongest assets are my communications skills and the ability to
quickly identify and resolve problems.

If you are interested in a Credit and Collection Manager with a proven
track record, let's meet and discuss how I can utilize my skills to meet
Baker Products' needs.

Thank you for your interest.

Sincerely,

Jonathan Riley

Encl.

October 4, 1993

Better Industries
45 Second Avenue
Chicago, IL 60611

Dear Ms. Hemmingway:

   I am very interested in the Chief Financial Officer opportunity as adver-
tized in the Chicago Tribune.

   My educational and work experiences are primarily in the financial and
accounting management area. I have experience in strategic and business planning, corporate development, financial planning and budgeting, forecasting,
and cash and tax management. As Chief Financial Officer for Universal Industries, I guide and direct the accounting and finance functions for an organization with approximately $75 million in annual revenue.

   My résumé is enclosed. I would welcome the opportunity to further discuss
my qualifications for employment at Better Industries. Please feel free to
contact me at your convenience. Thank you for your time and consideration. I
look forward to your response.

Sincerely,

Susan Logan

enc.

Comments

October 4, 1993

Better Industries
45 Second Avenue
Chicago, IL 60611

Dear Ms. Hemmingway:

①

② I am very interested in the Chief Financial Officer opportunity as adver-
tized in the <u>Chicago Tribune.</u>

③
My educational and work experiences are primarily in the financial and
accounting management area. I have experience in strategic and business planning, corporate development, financial planning and budgeting, forecasting,
④ and cash and tax management. As Chief Financial Officer for Universal Industries, I guide and direct the accounting and finance functions for an organization with approximately $75 million in annual revenue.

My résumé is enclosed. I would welcome the opportunity to further discuss
my qualifications for employment at Better Industries. Please feel free to ⑤
contact me at your convenience. Thank you for your time and consideration. I
look forward to your response.

Sincerely,

Susan Logan

enc.

1. Try not to begin with an *I*.
2. Typo.
3. Are you qualified for the position? If so, state it.
4. This is good but should be separate.
5. Split this into two paragraphs. Too many short, choppy sentences.

Comments

The paragraphs are too thick and hide your qualifications. Emphasize by dividing the qualifications into separate paragraphs.

9445 Marley Lane
Chicago, Illinois 60600
(312) 455-XXXX

October 4, 1993

Better Industries
45 Second Avenue
Chicago, IL 60611

Dear Ms. Hemmingway:

The Chief Financial Officer position you advertised in the <u>Chicago Tribune</u> is exactly the opportunity I've been looking for.

My broad financial and accounting management experience qualifies me for this position, as outlined in the enclosed résumé.

I am highly skilled in **strategic** and **business planning, corporate development, financial planning** and **budgeting, forecasting,** and **cash and tax management**.

As Chief Financial Officer, I guide and direct the accounting and finance functions for Universal Industries, an organization with annual revenues of $75 million.

My experience enables me to make a contribution to your organization. I would like the opportunity to further discuss my qualifications for employment at Better Industries.

Thank you for your time and consideration. I look forward to your response.

Sincerely,

Susan Logan

Encl.

April 12, 1993

San Francisco General
1667 Main Street
San Francisco, CA 94108

Dear Mr. Littlejohn:

I am currently seeking a position as Nursing Director and am interested in pursuing any opportunities within your hospital.

Presently, I manage and supervise nursing activities for a 210-bed hospital. My chief responsibilities are to oversee and provide administrative support for 10 inpatient units and emergency room while supervising a staff of 22 RNs and 43 paraprofessionals.

I have been recognized for my success in motivating staff to achieve organizational goals while continuing to provide optimal customer care.

I would like to meet with you and discuss your present and future staffing needs. I'll call you to set up an appointment.

Thank you for your time and consideration.

Yours truly,

Jaycee Ritter

Encl.

April 12, 1993

San Francisco General
1667 Main Street
San Francisco, CA 94108

Dear Mr. Littlejohn:

   I am currently seeking a position as Nursing Director and am interested in pursuing <u>any opportunities</u> within your hospital.

   Presently, I manage and supervise nursing activities for a 210-bed hospital. My chief responsibilities are to oversee and provide administrative support for 10 inpatient units and emergency room while supervising a staff of 22 RNs and 43 paraprofessionals.

   I have been recognized for my success in motivating staff to achieve organizational goals while continuing to provide optimal customer care.

   I would like to meet with you and discuss your present and future staffing needs. I'll call you to set up an appointment.

   Thank you for your time and consideration.

Yours truly,

Jaycee Ritter

Encl.

1. Too vague. Needs a stronger opening.
2. The sentence structure is awkward.
3. This is good. Build on it.
4. This is good but can be strengthened.

Comments
Begin with more punch, and elaborate on qualifications and what you can do for the employer.

96 Foggy Court
San Francisco, California 94100
(415) 838-XXXX

April 12, 1993

San Francisco General
1667 Main Street
San Francisco, CA 94108

Dear Mr. Littlejohn:

If your hospital would benefit from a dynamic, motivated nursing professional with a management background in health care delivery systems, I think you will find my qualifications interesting.

I now manage and supervise nursing activities for a 210-bed hospital, overseeing and providing administrative support for 10 inpatient units and emergency room while supervising 22 RNs and 43 paraprofessionals.

My recent performance appraisals characterize me as:

"Highly successful in motivating staff to achieve organizational goals while providing optimal customer care."

"Recognized specialist in managing multiple and diverse assignments, handling patient problems and personnel conflicts with ease."

I would like to meet and discuss your present and future needs. My nursing expertise and management skills will enable me to make a positive contribution to your hospital.

I look forward to speaking with you.

Yours truly,

Jaycee Ritter

Encl.

December 2, 1993

Southern Print, Inc.
78 Granite Street
Winston-Salem, NC 27108

Dear Ms. Shallo:

I am seeking a position that will use my extensive experience and skills as a Graphic designer and illustrator. I prefer a demanding workload and an employer who is interested in creative, high-quality products.

My background includes over 5 years of experience in Macintosh desktop publishing and design. My employer has consistently praised the high quality of my products. My strongest assets are my drawing ability, keen graphic sense, and a natural aptitude for design composition. Because of my excellent communication skills, I can make highly technical information and ideas understandable for targeted audiences.

My last employer has undergone downsizing due to budget cuts. I am a hard worker with a proven track record. The attached résumé, samples, and references reflect the level and variety of my capabilities. I welcome an opportunity to meet with you in person to discuss becoming part of your team.

Sincerely,

Les Cripp

Enclosures

December 2, 1993

Southern Print, Inc.
78 Granite Street
Winston-Salem, NC 27108

Dear Ms. Shallo:

    I am seeking a position that will use my extensive experience and skills ② as a Graphic designer and illustrator. I prefer a demanding workload and an employer who is interested in creative, high-quality products.

    My background includes over 5 years of experience in Macintosh desktop publishing and design. My employer has consistently praised the high quality of my products. My strongest assets are my drawing ability, keen graphic sense, and a natural aptitude for design composition. Because of my excellent communication skills, I can make highly technical information and ideas understandable for targeted audiences.

    My last employer has undergone downsizing due to budget cuts. I am a hard worker with a proven track record. The attached résumé, samples, and references reflect the level and variety of my capabilities. I welcome an opportunity to meet with you in person to discuss becoming part of your team.

Sincerely,

Les Cripp

Enclosures

1. This word shouldn't be capitalized unless you also capitalize *designer* and *illustrator.*
2. This term is awkward. Rephrase.
3. Spell out numbers 1 through 10. See basic number rules on page 6.
4. Good information. Split up for more emphasis.
5. Awkward construction. Rewrite.
6. Omit, it's negative.
7. It's not appropriate to send references. Wait until you're a job candidate.
8. Good close. Split for better emphasis.

Comments
Good information that needs to be sharpened. Demonstrate your desktop publishing skills when producing your letter.

LES CRIPP

45 Winding Way
Winston-Salem, North Carolina 27108
(919) 888-XXX

December 2, 1993

Southern Print, Inc.
78 Granite Street
Winston-Salem, NC 27108

Dear Ms. Shallo:

Could you use a graphic designer and illustrator who thrives in a fast-paced, demanding environment while producing creative, high-quality products?

My background includes over five years of experience in Macintosh desktop publishing and design. My strengths are my drawing ability, keen graphic sense, and a natural aptitude for design composition. I use effective communication skills to make highly technical information and ideas understandable to targeted audiences.

My employer has consistently praised the high quality of my products. The attached résumé and samples reflect the level and variety of my capabilities.

I would like to meet with you in person and discuss becoming a part of your team. I will call to schedule an appointment.

Thank you for your time and consideration.

Sincerely,

Les Cripp

Enclosures

October 3, 1993

Western Manufacturers
44 First Street
Los Angeles, CA 90012

Dear Sir:

This is in response to your advertisement for a Senior Contracts Administrator in the October 3rd edition of the <u>Los Angeles Times.</u>

For the last ten years, I have worked in the high-tech industry in the
financial departments. I have been given increasingly responsible positions
and have always enjoyed the reputation of a dedicated team player who gets the
job done.

My credentials include:

o Bachelor of Science degree in Business Administration
o Master's degree in Business Administration
o Six years of experience in budget preparation and
   financial analysis
o Four years' experience in contract administration
o Five years' experience in proposal preparation and
   negotiation
o Hands- on experience with Lotus, WordPerfect, and other software
   programs
o Working knowledge of FAR and DAR

Throughout my career my superiors have recognized and rewarded my personal
commitment and ability to meet whatever objectives were assigned.

I have enclosed a résumé which provides a fairly complete summary of my
education and experience. I would enjoy the chance to explore employment opportunities with your company. I can be reached at (310) 883-XXXX.

Sincerely,

Walter Woods

Enc.

Comments

October 3, 1993

Western Manufacturers
44 First Street
Los Angeles, CA 90012

Dear Sir: ①   ②

    This is in response to your advertisement for a Senior Contracts Adminis-
trator in the October 3rd <u>edition</u> of the <u>Los Angeles Times.</u>

                           ③
④ ──── For the last ten years, I have worked in the high-tech industry in the
financial departments. I have been given increasingly responsible positions
and have always enjoyed the reputation of a dedicated team player who gets the
job done.

    My credentials include:

    o Bachelor of Science degree in Business Administration ⑤
    o Master's degree in Business Administration
    o Six years of experience in budget preparation and
       financial analysis
    o Four years' experience in contract administration
    o Five years' experience in proposal preparation and
       negotiation ⑥
⑦ ──── o Hands-|on experience with Lotus, WordPerfect, and other software
       programs
    o Working knowledge of FAR and DAR

                    ⑧
    Throughout my career|my superiors have recognized and rewarded my personal ⎫
commitment and ability to meet whatever objectives were assigned.   ⎬ ⑨
                                                                               ⎭

    I have enclosed a résumé which provides a fairly complete summary of my
education and experience. I would enjoy the chance to explore employment opportunities with your company. I can be reached at (310) 883-XXXX.

Sincerely,

Walter Woods

Enc.

1. If the reader is a woman, she'll be turned off immediately. Try *Dear Employer.*
2. The first paragraph is a poor choice for an opening. What does *this* refer to?
3. Unnecessary.
4. Tighten this up.
5. I wouldn't include your undergraduate degree. Begin with your Master's; it's more impressive.
6. Are you good at it? If so, state expertise.
7. Take out the extra space.
8. Punctuation. Add a comma.
9. Good idea, but rewrite so that you don't sound overly confident.

Comments

Don't flatter yourself too much. State clearly and concisely why you're qualified.

574 Third Avenue
Culver City, California 90230
(310) 883-XXXX

October 3, 1993

Western Manufacturers
44 First Street
Los Angeles, CA 90012

Dear Employer:

My extensive contract administration experience makes me highly qualified for the Senior Contracts Administrator position you advertised in the October 3rd Los Angeles Times.

Ten years of financial experience in the high-tech industry have earned me the reputation of being a dedicated team player who gets the job done. My efforts have been rewarded with increased responsibility.

My credentials include:

• Master's degree in Business Administration
• Six years' experience in budget preparation and financial analysis
• Four years' experience in contract administration
• Expertise in proposal preparation and negotiation
• Hands-on experience with Lotus 1-2-3, WordPerfect, and other software programs
• Working knowledge of FAR and DAR

Throughout my career, my supervisors have consistently recognized my personal commitment and ability to meet all assigned objectives.

The enclosed résumé outlines my education and experience. I would like to meet with you to explore employment opportunities with your company. I can be reached at (310) 883-XXXX and look forward to hearing from you.

Sincerely,

Walter Woods

Encl.

February 7, 1994

Dear Sir or Madam,

   I am writing to express my interest in obtaining the Health Service Coordinator position. Please review the attached copy of my résumé. If you feel
that my experience would be an asset to your organization, then I welcome the
opportunity to meet with you in person.

                        Sincerely,

                        Cynthia Small

February 7, 1994

①

Dear Sir or Madam, ②

    I am writing to express my interest in obtaining the Health Service Coor-
dinator position. Please review the attached copy of my résumé. If you feel
that my experience would be an asset to your organization, then I welcome the
opportunity to meet with you in person.

                               Sincerely, ③

                               Cynthia Small

④

1. Your letter needs to be directed to an organization and individual.
2. Incorrect punctuation. Use a colon (:).
3. The letter doesn't follow any accepted business format.
4. Missing *Enclosure*.

Comments

This letter is impersonal and too short. It doesn't indicate that it's responding to an employment advertisement. Even if the résumé closely matches the requested requirements, the poor letter will knock the sender out of the running.

83 Fourth Street
Philadelphia, PA 19120
(215) 733-XXXX

February 7, 1994

Health Plus
99 Federal Street
Philadelphia, PA 19122

Dear Employer:

The Health Services Coordinator position advertised through the National Association of Health Care Administrators is an excellent match for my skills and experience.

My qualifications are ideal for the position you describe. I have extensive **provider relations** experience with an **HMO/PPO**. For the past three years, I have **serviced and negotiated contracts** with a **managed care program**. I'm **highly skilled in both oral and written communications**. The enclosed résumé provides further details of my experience, training, and skills.

I am very interested in this position and would appreciate the opportunity to discuss my background and your requirements in greater detail.

I look forward to hearing from you.

Sincerely,

Cynthia Small

Encl.

74 Lawyers Road NW
Vienna, VA 22180
(703) 938-XXXX

To Whom It May Concern:

I am very interested in a career with your company as a Development Director.
The enclosed résumé will furnish you with information concerning my background
and qualifications.

I look forward to having the opportunity of a personal interview to discuss the
future.

Please contact me at the above address and phone number.

                              Thank you,

                              Theresa Diaz

Encl. Résumé

① 74 Lawyers Road NW
Vienna, VA 22180
(703) 938-XXXX
                                    ②

To Whom It May Concern:

I am very interested in a career with your company as a Development Director.
The enclosed résumé will furnish you with information concerning my background
and qualifications. ③

I look forward to having the opportunity of a personal interview to discuss the
future. ④

Please contact me at the above address and phone number. ⑤

                                Thank you, ⑥

                                Theresa Diaz

Encl. Résumé

1. This is not the correct place for your address. You *must* follow an acceptable business format. And don't forget the date!
2. A blind letter like this will get action—right into the wastepaper basket! Your letter must be addressed and directed to a specific individual.
3. You must tell an employer what you can offer.
4. Why would they want to discuss the future?
5. It's up to you to take the initiative to pursue an opportunity.
6. Incorrect complimentary close. Use *Sincerely, Sincerely yours,* or *Truly yours.*

Comments
Unsolicited letters must be directed to someone's attention. They need to make a statement about your qualifications and must interest someone in wanting to meet you.

74 Lawyers Road NW
Vienna, VA 22180
(703) 938-XXXX

August 23, 1993

National Rights for the Arts
Ms. White, Director
1331 P Street N.W.
Washington, D.C. 20002

Dear Ms. White:

    The ability to approach problems as opportunities and develop innovative solutions has resulted in my rapid career growth and a desire to take on new challenges.

    I am interested in utilizing my fund-raising expertise in a Director of Development position. As outlined in my enclosed résumé, I have progressive experience in raising funds and in successfully coordinating special events.

    In my current position as Assistant Development Director, I thrive in a fast-paced environment, handling multiple jobs simultaneously while consistently meeting deadlines and financial objectives.

    Career growth and challenge are my goals. If you are looking for a seasoned fundraiser, I would welcome the opportunity to focus my energies in making a valuable contribution to the National Rights for the Arts. I can be reached at (703) 938-XXXX and look forward to speaking with you.

Sincerely,

Theresa Diaz

Enclosure

September 15, 1993

Capital Construction Corporation
7889 Wisconsin Avenue
Bethesda, MD 20814

Dear Sir or Madam:

   Enclosed please find my Résumé for consideration in filling the position of Executive Assistant. In my capacity of Executive Assistant to the Chief Operating Officer of a publicly held software company, I have utilized excellent organizational, written and oral communication skills to provide executive secretarial support. In addition, I have developed skills in using word processing, database, and spreadsheet applications.

   I would welcome the opportunity to personally meet with your representatives to further discuss the Executive Assistant position, and look forward to hearing from you in this regard.

Sincerely,

Ramona Kone

Enc.

Comments

September 15, 1993

Capital Construction Corporation
7889 Wisconsin Avenue
Bethesda, MD 20814

Dear Sir or Madam: ①
                          ②

    Enclosed please find my Résumé for consideration in filling the position
of Executive Assistant. In my capacity of Executive Assistant to the Chief
Operating Officer of a publicly held software company, I have utilized excellent organizational, written and oral communication skills to provide executive secretarial support. In addition, I have developed skills in using word
processing, database, and spreadsheet applications.   } ③

    I would welcome the opportunity to personally meet with your repre-
sentatives to further discuss the Executive Assistant position, and look forward to hearing from you in this regard.
                          ④

Sincerely,

Ramona Kone

Enc.

Comments

1. Use a more contemporary salutation. Try calling the organization to identify the individual who will be screening the letters.
2. Weak opening. *Résumé* shouldn't be capitalized.
3. These points are all important but they're buried here. Highlight them by formatting in one or two paragraphs.
4. Stiff and wordy.

Comments

Executive Assistants compose and format correspondence. This letter must be a sample of your work. Make it contemporary and concise while highlighting the desired skills.

76 Sugar Hill Lane
Wheaton, Maryland 20900
(301) 689-XXXX

September 15, 1993

Capital Construction Corporation
Ms. Karey, Personnel Director
7889 Wisconsin Avenue
Bethesda, MD 20814

Dear Ms. Karey:

If you're looking for a self-starting Executive Assistant with maturity, tact, discretion, an eye for detail, and the ability to work well with a variety of personalities, please consider my credentials for the position.

My five years of executive/administrative assistant experience have developed skills in:

- Organization
- Written and oral communications
- Word processing, database, and spreadsheet applications

Most recently these skills were used to provide executive secretarial support to the Chief Operating Officer of a publicly held software company.

I would be interested in meeting with you to discuss how I can support your organization's needs. I will call you to set up an appointment.

Sincerely,

Ramona Kone

Encl.

January 13, 1994

The Greasy Spoon
44 Federal Highway
Columbus, OH 43215

Dear Sir:

I am responding to your ad for a Restaurant Manager as advertised in today's <u>Columbus Dispatch.</u>

I offer a variety of restaurant management experience including hiring, training, and supervising staffs of 28-30. As you an see from my résumé, I have worked with prominent restaurants, such as the Silver Dollar Restaurant.

I have reduced staff turnover and stabilized the work force by promoting from within, delegating responsibility, and recognizing performance. Additionally, I have increased sales by successfully coordinating local-store marketing and developing new products.

Recently, I established procedures for a new take-out/delivery system.

Please consider me a candidate for this position. I am available to meet with you to discuss the position.

Yours truly,

William Rhodes

Encl.

January 13, 1994

The Greasy Spoon
44 Federal Highway
Columbus, OH 43215

Dear Sir: ①

I am responding to your ad for a Restaurant Manager as advertised in today's ②
<u>Columbus Dispatch.</u>

I offer a variety of restaurant management experience including hiring, train- ③
ing, and supervising staffs of 28-30. As you an see from my résumé, I have
worked with <u>prominent restaurants,</u> such as the Silver Dollar Restaurant.
④
I have reduced staff turnover and stabilized the work force by promoting from ⎫
within, delegating responsibility, and recognizing performance. Addition-   ⎬ ⑤
ally, I have increased sales by successfully coordinating local-store market- ⎭
ing and developing new products.

Recently, I established procedures for a new take-out/delivery system. ⑥

Please consider me a candidate for this position. I am available to meet with
you to discuss the position. ⑦

Yours truly,

William Rhodes

Encl.

1. Use a more contemporary salutation.
2. Your opening is weak. Try something that will capture attention.
3. Shouldn't this be *can?*
4. This is overbearing. Let them see from your résumé what's prominent.
5. This is good, but try to list each accomplishment separately so that each one will stand out.
6. Include this with your other accomplishments.
7. Try to close by highlighting your special qualities. Think about what has made you successful in the restaurant business.

Comments

Lots of good experience and accomplishments. Format the letter more effectively so that these are clear. Strengthen your first and last paragraphs by listing your skills and what you can offer.

After

56 Grain Lane
Columbus, OH 43210
(614) 521-XXXX

January 13, 1994

The Greasy Spoon
44 Federal Highway
Columbus, OH 43215

Dear Employer:

My four years of experience in all facets of restaurant operations qualifies me for the Restaurant Manager position you advertised in today's Columbus Dispatch.

As Assistant Manager of the Silver Dollar Restaurant, I hired, trained,
and supervised staffs of 28-30. Selected accomplishments include:

- Reduced staff turnover and stabilized the workforce by promoting
  from within, delegating responsibility, and recognizing performance.
- Increased sales by successfully coordinating local-store marketing
  and developing new products.
- Established procedures for a new take-out/delivery system.

If you're seeking an innovative, organized manager with exceptional
people skills, please consider me a candidate. I am available to meet
with you to discuss how I can contribute to the success of your operation.

Yours truly,

William Rhodes

Encl.

TO: National Industries
           Attn: Vice President, Administration
           58 Duke Lane
           Darien, CT 06820

FROM: Sandy Springfellow

DATE: March 1, 1994

Enclosed is a copy of my résumé. I am seeking employment as a Customer Service
Supervisor.

I have extensive experience in the field of customer service. I believe that
my résumé offers a good description of my work history, job interest, and qualifications. I would be happy to discuss any aspects of my work to anyone interested, and I encourage you to call my references.

                        Sincerely,

                        Sandy Springfellow

Comments

TO:　　　　National Industries
　　　　　　Attn: Vice President, Administration
　　　　　　58 Duke Lane
　　　　　　Darien, CT 06820

FROM:　　Sandy Springfellow

DATE:　　March 1, 1994

Enclosed is a copy of my résumé. I am seeking employment as a Customer Service
Supervisor. ②

I have extensive experience in the field of customer service. I believe that
my résumé offers a good description of my work history, job interest, and qualifications. I would be happy to discuss any aspects of my work to <u>anyone interested,</u> and I encourage you to call my references.

　　　　　　　　　　　　　　　　　　Sincerely,

　　　　　　　　　　　　　　　　　　Sandy Springfellow

1. You have used an incorrect interoffice memo format. It's inappropriate for external business correspondence.
2. Too blunt.
3. Give the employer a sample of what's in your résumé.
4. Too vague.
5. You don't want to be prescreened through your references, you want an interview.

Comments

Inappropriate and incorrect format. Use and follow appropriate business-letter guidelines.

855 Windy Court
Darien, CT 06820
(213) 588-XXXX

March 1, 1994

National Industries
Sharon Hammer
Vice President, Administration
58 Duke Lane
Darien, CT 06820

Dear Ms. Hammer:

Customers influence business outcomes. Satisfied customers generate re-
peat sales and new business and make the difference between profit and
loss.

I can help your organization satisfy your customers by working effectively with marketing, service, and administrative groups to ensure optimal customer support.

As a highly motivated, detail-oriented Customer Service Supervisor, I
have developed excellent skills in written and oral communications, prob-
lem-solving, and follow-up.

My recent performance evaluation states:

> "Customer satisfaction is at an all-time high. Exceptional perfor-
> mance by Sandy deserves credit for her excellent training, manage-
> ment, and follow-up of her people. Very quick to identify problem
> areas and takes good corrective measures to resolve them quickly."

I would like the opportunity to satisfy your customers and assist your
organization in reaching your goals. When would it be convenient for us
to meet?

                              Sincerely,

                              Sandy Springfellow

Encl.

June 3, 1993

Cutting Edge Computers, Inc.
Attn: Personnel Director
99 Main Street
Piscataway, NJ 08854

Gentlemen:

I am responding to your need for a Computer Sales Representative as advertised in the June 1 <u>Star-Ledger.</u>

I offer a varied combination of abilities and experience that would make me an asset to your staff. As you can see from my résumé, I have four years of sales experience. I am highly skilled in identifying revenue opportunities, prioritizing accounts, and developing action plans.

While my experience is in the telecommunications field, I feel my skills can easily transfer to the computer industry.

Thank you for taking the time to review my qualifications and I look forward to meeting you to further discuss my qualifications.

Sincerely,

Frank French

enc.

June 3, 1993

Cutting Edge Computers, Inc.
Attn: Personnel Director
99 Main Street
Piscataway, NJ 08854

Gentlemen: ①

    I am responding to your need for a Computer Sales Representative as advertised in the June 1 <u>Star-Ledger.</u>

②

    I offer a varied combination of <u>abilities and experience</u> that would make ③ me an asset to your staff. As you can see from my résumé, I have four years of sales experience. I am highly skilled in identifying revenue opportunities, prioritizing accounts, and developing action plans. ④

    While my experience is in the telecommunications field, I feel my skills can easily transfer to the computer industry. ⑤

⑥   Thank you for taking the time to review my qualifications and I look forward to meeting you to further discuss my qualifications.

Sincerely,

Frank French

enc.

1. Be more contemporary. *Dear Personnel Director* is better. Even better, call and find out the name of the Personnel Director.
2. Too many *I*'s. Sounds self-serving.
3. Like what?
4. This is good and should be developed.
5. You must present a better case of why someone should hire you.
6. How will you meet? Use a better close.

Comments

When changing industries, present a good case for why someone should take a chance and hire you. Focus on skills that transfer and how you can make a contribution.

65 Columbia Court
Trenton, NJ 08068
(609) 622-XXXX

June 3, 1993

Cutting Edge Computers, Inc.
Attn: Personnel Director
99 Main Street
Piscataway, NJ 08854

Dear Mr. Jeffries:

   Your advertisement for a Computer Sales Representative in the June
1st Star-Ledger describes exactly the position I am seeking.

   My four years of sales experience qualify me for this position. I am
highly skilled in identifying revenue opportunities, prioritizing accounts, and developing action plans.

   I consistently achieved 120-175% of my sales objectives by persever-
ing, overcoming objections, and successfully closing sales.

   While my experience has been in the telecommunications industry, I
have had a long-term interest in computers and would like the opportunity
to transfer my solid sales skills while diligently learning the computer
industry.

   It's impossible to convey my interest, enthusiasm, and positive
spirit on paper. I'd like to meet with you and demonstrate my desire and
ability to take on this challenging position.

   I look forward to hearing from you.

Sincerely,

Frank French

Encl.

October 4, 1993

Controller
Box 66
c/o Des Moines Register
Des Moines, IA 50311

Dear Financial Officers:

I am forwarding a copy of my résumé in consideration for the Assistant Controller career opening you are seeking to fill.

I want to share with you how I will be an asset to your hospitality team. Due to the structure of XYZ's Inn, my previous career positions were not titled Assistant Controller as such. However, the routine property-level accounting tasks were performed by on-site managers. As a Front Office Manager, I supervised managers in A/R, A/P, and reservation collections. In addition, I performed monthly petty cash, bank account, and credit card reconciliations. This experience will follow me as to my new career with your hotel.

Before I became Office Manager, I held a position as Auditor while finishing my accounting degree. This position allowed me to excel in many software applications. I was able to apply my advanced macro programming knowledge of Lotus 123 and Symphony to build a fully automated budget variance and cost reporting system for the hotel. This also required DOS batch file creation to form a menu-driven environment to interface with OLIVE, XYZ's corporate reservation system. I seek to bring this same challenge-meeting approach to your firm.

As a CPA candidate seeking a hospitality career in the Des Moines area, I am eager to meet with you to further discuss how I can meet your department's needs. You may reach me during business hours at (515) 987-XXXX.

Thank you in advance for your consideration of my qualifications. I look forward to hearing from a member of your team!

Sincerely,

Gwendolyn Pine

Enclosure

October 4, 1993

Controller
Box 66
c/o Des Moines Register
Des Moines, IA 50311

Dear Financial Officers:

I am forwarding a copy of my résumé in consideration for the Assistant Controller career opening you are seeking to fill.

I want to share with you how I will be an asset to your hospitality team. Due
to the structure of XYZ's Inn, my previous career positions were not titled
Assistant Controller as such. However, the routine property-level accounting
tasks were performed by on-site managers. As a Front Office Manager, I supervised managers in A/R, A/P, and reservation collections. In addition, I performed monthly petty cash, bank account, and credit card reconciliations. This
experience will follow me as to my new career with your hotel.

Before I became Office Manager, I held a position as Auditor while finishing
my accounting degree. This position allowed me to excel in many software applications. I was able to apply my advanced macro programming knowledge of
Lotus 123 and Symphony to build a fully automated budget variance and cost
reporting system for the hotel. This also required DOS batch file creation to
form a menu-driven environment to interface with OLIVE, XYZ's corporate reservation system. I seek to bring this same challenge-meeting approach to your
firm.

As a CPA candidate seeking a hospitality career in the Des Moines area, I am
eager to meet with you to further discuss how I can meet your department's
needs. You may reach me during business hours at (515) 987-XXXX.

Thank you in advance for your consideration of my qualifications. I look forward to hearing from a member of your team!

Sincerely,

Gwendolyn Pine

Enclosure

1. Too many *I*'s.
2. Use *position* instead.
3. This statement takes away from your experience. Rather, match your experience to the requirements.
4. Too much extraneous information takes away from what you have to offer.
5. There are real skills and accomplishments here but they're buried. Simplify and bring them out.
6. Incorrect spelling.

Comments

Paragraphs are too thick. There's too much information that not only doesn't add to credentials but diminishes them. Make your letter more concise, and highlight specific qualifications that relate to the position.

89 Lovell Lane, Des Moines, Iowa 50300

October 4, 1993

Controller
Box 66
c/o Des Moines Register
Des Moines, IA 50311

Dear Employer:

Your recent ad for an Assistant Controller in the Des Moines Register is
an exact fit for my qualifications and industry experience.

My current responsibilities, background, and skills, as outlined in the
enclosed résumé, parallel the job requirements listed:

- As financial manager with XYZ's Inn, supervise managers in A/R,
  A/P, and reservation collections.
- Perform monthly petty cash, bank account, and credit card reconcil-
  iations.
- Have expertise in accounting software applications and a technical
  ability and talent for solving systems problems.
- Am a CPA candidate.

At XYZ's Inn, I developed a fully automated budget variance and cost reporting system for the hotel by applying advanced macro programming techniques using Lotus 1-2-3 and Symphony. The project required creating DOS
batch files to form a menu-driven environment to interface with OLIVE,
XYZ's corporate reservation system.

I'm interested in building a financial management career within the hospitality industry, and the position you advertised is exactly the challenge I'm seeking. I'm eager to meet with you to discuss how I can
satisfy your organization's needs. You can reach me at (515) 987-XXXX.

I look forward to hearing from you.

Sincerely yours,

Gwendolyn Pine

Enclosure

                          Bert Washington
             65 Walnut Hill, Huntsville, Alabama 35805
             (205) 333-XXXX (Off)   (205) 876-XXXX (Res.)

Dear Personnel Director:

The accompanying résumé is submitted for your consideration, and I hope you
will find it deserving of your attention. This résumé briefly describes my
qualifications, but by no means reflects my total capabilities.

I would like to explore the possibility of joining your organization as an
addition to your administrative or managerial staff. My experience, education,
and interpersonal skills would make me an ideal candidate for this position.

In closing, let me take this opportunity to express my sincere thanks for your
valuable time and consideration in this important career opportunity. I would
like to talk to you at your convenience to discuss in greater detail how my
experience could be of mutual benefit. I look forward to hearing from you.

Sincerely,

Bert Washington

Résumé Enclosed

Comments

Bert Washington
65 Walnut Hill, Huntsville, Alabama 35805
(205) 333-XXXX (Off) (205) 876-XXXX (Res.)
①

Dear Personnel Director: ②

③

The accompanying résumé is submitted for your consideration, and <u>I hope you</u>
④ <u>will find it deserving</u> of your attention. This résumé briefly describes my
qualifications, but by no means reflects my total capabilities.

I would like to explore the possibility of joining your organization as an
addition to your administrative or managerial staff. My experience, education, ⑤
and interpersonal skills would make me an ideal candidate for <u>this position.</u> ⑥

In closing, let me take this opportunity to express my sincere <u>thanks for your</u>
⑦ <u>valuable time</u> and consideration in this important career opportunity. I would
like to talk to you at your convenience to discuss in greater detail how my
experience could be of mutual benefit. I look forward to hearing from you.

Sincerely, ⑧

Bert Washington

Résumé Enclosed ⑨

1. Odd abbreviations.
2. Letter must be directed to a specific individual.
3. Poor beginning. Your letter should spark some interest, not introduce your résumé.
4. Sounds as if you're not confident of your qualifications.
5. What position? What area? Too vague.
6. What position?
7. No one will spend time considering a vague, unfocused letter.
8. There's no indication of what the experience is.
9. Why highlight by boldfacing this?

Comments

This is a mass-produced "broadcast" letter. It's written for everyone and appeals to no one. Letters must be targeted and directed for specific jobs and to specific individuals.

Bert Washington
65 Walnut Hill, Huntsville, Alabama 35805
(205) 333-XXXX (Office) (205) 876-XXXX (Home)

November 19, 1993

DEF Corporation
Mr. Malcolm Fife
Vice President/Controller
432 Colby Drive
Huntsville, AL 35805

Dear Mr. Fife:

Do you believe that leading, motivating, and training employees promotes enthusiasm, makes the workplace enjoyable, and invigorates the bottom line? If so, we have a lot in common and should explore developing a relationship.

My five years of administrative experience in a technical environment has developed skills in budget and financial reporting practices, overseeing performance review programs, and monitoring and supervising staffing needs, requirements, and assignments. I have excellent interpersonal and communication skills and can quickly develop rapport at all staff levels.

Most recently, I directed facility modifications and coordinated two office moves--efficiently, effectively, and on time.

I would like to discuss with you how I can apply my administrative expertise to an Assistant Division Administrator position with DEF Corporation. I will call you to set up an appointment.

I look forward to speaking with you.

Sincerely,

Bert Washington

Encl.